WHAT'S NEXT
FOR YOU

The Eightfold Path to Transforming the
Way We Hire and Manage Talent

A S H U T O S H   G A R G
and
K A M A L   A H L U W A L I A

BALBOA.
PRESS
A DIVISION OF HAY HOUSE

Balboa Press books may be ordered through booksellers or by contacting:

Balboa Press
A Division of Hay House
1663 Liberty Drive
Bloomington, IN 47403
www.balboapress.com
1 (877) 407-4847

Print information available on the last page.

ISBN: 978-1-9822-2546-9 (sc)
ISBN: 978-1-9822-2548-3 (hc)
ISBN: 978-1-9822-2547-6 (e)

Library of Congress Control Number: 2019903946

Balboa Press rev. date: 05/09/2019

What's Next For You:
The Eightfold Path To Transforming The Way
We Hire And Manage Talent

Ashutosh Garg & Kamal Ahluwalia, Eightfold

Foreword by John W. Thompson

*To my wife Shilpi who has chosen to be behind
the scenes, do all the work, and let me live
my dream.
To my parents, Harish and Usha, and brother
Paritosh whose love and support has been a constant
pillar in my life. To my kids, Avyand and Ayansh,
who I wish I could spend more time with every
day, who have brought in a new meaning to life.
— Ashu*

*To my parents Awtar and Darshan, thank you
for everything. It is a privilege to have
great parents.
To my wife Parveen, and my kids Meha and
Manak, you inspire me to do my best everyday.
Meha and Manak: what is next for you?
— Kamal*

*To Kristin Marguerite Doidge — without you,
this book would not be possible. Thank you.
— Ashu & Kamal*

CONTENTS

Foreword

FOREWORD

Every industry is being disrupted by new technology, new business models and ever-increasing customer expectations. Companies driving this disruption are rapidly becoming market leaders and others are trying their best to react and keep up. Whatever it is you're building or selling, it's a safe bet that your current and future employees have very different expectations from you as well.

With over 40 years of enterprise leadership and entrepreneurial experience, I know firsthand how important strong talent is when it comes to growing a business.

Scaling a business is hard — and requires the perfect mix of winning strategy, culture, and the right people in the right roles. Transforming a business already at scale — that's even harder.

I've held many different leadership roles throughout my years of working within the technology sector, from my current role as Chairman of Microsoft to a decade spent as Chairman/CEO of Symantec, and almost 30 years at IBM. Along the way, I've had the incredible opportunity to advise dozens of entrepreneurs with amazing ideas and have helped companies not only survive disruptive technology transitions, but use them as change agents to accelerate their own evolution.

Businesses are having to adapt to technology changes and changes in customer expectations roughly every 10 years — a timeframe that is continuing to shrink.

As a result, business leaders need to really focus on rethinking their business strategy and the associated talent strategy so they have the organizational capability to transform and capitalize on the inevitable technology shifts.

The same can be said of navigating through major technology shifts, which is why Ashutosh and Kamal's book couldn't come at a better time.

Finding and hiring the best talent in the market, retaining and growing your existing talent and building a diverse workforce are all very much inter-related issues.

Millennials will be 50% of our entire workforce globally within 5 years. It's obvious this demographic has a passion for technology as users. But, it's also obvious they have a very different view of life and career, and don't have any qualms about job hopping, which only expedites the rapid turnover of top talent.

We have to make sure, as leaders, that the environment we create is not just welcoming, but that new hires want to stay with us for a longer period of time. When it's the norm for new hires to leave after 18 months, we have a serious challenge.

It's necessary to have a meaningful discussion of the value of continuity for all employees as we shift our thinking on how to effectively incorporate our up-and-coming talent into the fold.

Many of our current legacy enterprise applications were built for the company — not for the employees or candidates. Eightfold is finally providing an Artificial Intelligence or AI-powered platform that allows the individual — millennial, Gen X, and Gen Y alike — to map out their careers, learn new skills and grow with the company.

With Eightfold AI, you can do this at scale in a self-service mode, which is very different than what we have been able to do in the past. This will allow employees to stay aligned with a company's business objectives, grow and change their careers as life dictates, and have the continuity that we all need to realize our potential. I'm really excited about this new approach and ability to solve it at scale.

As the title of the book suggests, we need to make sure our valued employees always know "what's next."

A rhetoric of fear often surrounds the rapid pace of technological advancement. People fear their jobs will be replaced by a machine or that new software will be so disruptive that human minds will no longer be able to keep up.

We often forget technology has already had a profound disruption on the job market and it is up to us to decide how we will marshal the new systems and capabilities.

What Eightfold is doing is a supremely unique, universally applicable way to solve this talent gap with AI and machine learning.

The Eightfold Talent Intelligence Platform system will help CEOs and CHROs build the teams they need to drive and sustain the digital transformation in their companies. If they are talking about digital transformation, they now need to be talking about talent transformation as well.

But it's clear we can't await for those transitions to find us — we must rise to meet them now.

We read headlines and hear complaints about the talent crisis so often it has almost become commonplace. But, these statistics present the harsh reality of today's talent crisis. CEOs and CHROs aren't really sure how to remedy the problem.

Eightfold's 2018 Talent Intelligence Report shows that 28% of the jobs that are currently open will not be filled in the next 12 months. Nearly 50% of top talent want to leave their jobs within the first two years of being hired. This indicates the time to rethink our talent strategy is now.

I myself have experienced these challenges firsthand as a CEO and advisor to numerous startups and large enterprises. Employers understand that having top talent is a key part of any successful business, yet they too often struggle or fail to keep the best people around.

Those who are early adopters of this valuable talent platform will be the ones that will be impacted most positively by what Eightfold is doing.

The time to act is right now. What are you waiting for?

— John W. Thompson, Venture Partner, Lightspeed Venture Partners

About the
Authors

∞

ABOUT THE AUTHORS

Based in Mountain View, California, we've built Eightfold. ai, a company revolutionizing the talent management space through its patented artificial intelligence–based platform designed to empower enterprises to turn talent management into a competitive advantage. It was built by top engineers out of Facebook, Google and other leading technology companies.

My name is Ashutosh Garg, and I am the Chief Executive Officer and Cofounder of Eightfold. I've worked in Silicon Valley for decades, researching and implementing machine learning technology. Previously, I worked at Google for more than four years (which is eons in Silicon Valley!), where I led search and personalization efforts, and did the same for IBM.

In 2009, I founded Bloomreach, a leading vendor for Digital Experience Platforms, aiming to optimize businesses' online platforms to drive conversion.

It's no coincidence we're working on this revolution in Silicon Valley. The tech capital of the world — perhaps best known for its innovative companies and a few genius startup founders who only wear T-shirts — has some of the highest attrition rates in the country.

On average, employees stay fewer than two years, compared to the already low 4.2 years nationally.

Throughout my career, I've witnessed this attrition firsthand. I realized something had to change. I decided to combine my knowledge of AI technology and experience building great teams to help people find meaningful work, and in turn reduce employee turnover. After meeting Varun Kacholia at Google, we decided to team up to create Eightfold.

Kamal Ahluwalia, who joins me in writing this book, serves as the President at Eightfold. He brings extensive experience in building great teams and affecting change at scale.

His leadership style – and ultimately, Eightfold's own company culture — has been transformed by the "Extreme Ownership" doctrine practiced by US Navy Seals. As Chief Revenue Officer at Apttus, Kamal led the company to market leadership in multiple product categories ahead of Salesforce, Oracle, SAP, and IBM. Prior to his role at Apttus, Kamal held various leadership positions at Selectica, Oracle and Apple.

Varun Kacholia, our Chief Technology Officer and cofounder, is one of the world's leaders when it comes to search, ranking, and machine learning. After ranking No. 2 at the Indian Institute of Technology in 2000 and earning his Master's degree from the University of

California, Berkeley, Varun went on to lead the News Feed team at Facebook and the YouTube Search and Recommendations team at Google.

He's passionate about how AI can be applied to everyday life and really have a positive impact on people's lives.

Throughout our careers, we have seen companies fail to recognize people's full potential, which has, in turn, created a talent crisis. Our technology can change that. Eightfold helps companies find and match the right person to the right role at the right time and, for the first time, personalize the recommendations at scale.

Employees are a company's greatest asset. And Eightfold wants to ensure the right fit for your company each and every time — especially when it matters most.

Introduction

INTRODUCTION

I spoke at an event recently. I asked the audience to raise their hands if they have ever submitted their resume or filled out a job application — but never once heard back.

As you can probably guess, the majority of the room raised their hands.

Searching for — and obtaining — meaningful work is one of the most significant and rewarding challenges we face in life. And yet many of us are still using outdated technologies and tools to try to reach for the dreams we know we can achieve.

WE'RE IN CRISIS.

You may not realize it, but we are in the midst of a talent crisis.

Everyone — from Apple, Google and Facebook to banks, hospitals and grocery chains — is searching for talent.

We are in the midst of a talent crisis - Everyone is searching for talent

But nationally, America is facing a shortage of well-qualified, skilled candidates, costing our economy billions every year. In fact, it's now the No. 1 risk for businesses, according to a recent study.[1]

Individual companies are feeling the pressure to hire even those who are not a perfect fit for the job. Candidates applying for work are often misinformed about the role, or cannot see how to apply their skills to the right job.

---

[1] https://www.gartner.com/en/newsroom/press-releases/2019-01-17-gartner-survey-shows-global-talent-shortage-is-now-the-top-emerging-risk-facing-organizations

As of December 2018, there were the number of job openings reached a series high of 7.3 million, a rate of 4.7 percent, according to the Bureau of Labor Statistics.[2]

There are more than 7 million open jobs in the United States

Glassdoor estimated the unfilled jobs on their platform to cost the economy in $272.6 billion, in an analysis released in February 2017.

In the tech industry alone, they estimated these openings to be costing $20.1 billion.[3]

---

[2] https://www.bls.gov/news.release/jolts.nr0.htm
[3] Chamberlain, A. (2017, February 9). *What's the Value of America's Unfilled Jobs?* Retrieved from: https://www.glassdoor.com

Unemployment nationwide was 3.7 percent in November 2018, the lowest rate in nearly 50 years, according to the National Conference of State Legislatures.[4]

And the skills gap cost our economy $13 billion a month, or roughly $160 billion a year in 2014, according to a Centre for Economics and Business Research study. Not only did companies miss revenue from unfilled positions, but under- and unemployed people spent less, also slowing the economy.[5]

These numbers are staggering, and the more we dug into the problem, the more we realized that our approach to talent management over the past decades — if not centuries — has been flawed, and will absolutely not work going forward.

WHAT'S NEXT?

If our mission is to make the future of talent management possible right now, we realized each of the following specific challenges would need to be addressed:

1. Resumes are bad and job descriptions are even worse, so we are fixing both.

2. People don't leave their current job to do the same thing in their next role, so it's very important to

---

[4] National Conference of State Legislatures. (2018, December 7). *National Employment Monthly Update.* Retrieved from: http://www.ncsl.org

[5] Centre for Economics and Business Research & Indeed. (2014, November). *The economic cost of unfilled jobs in the U.S.* Retrieved from: https://www.indeed.com/

understand "what's next" for an individual based on their capabilities.

3. If companies don't improve their talent retention practices, they will never be able to hire their way to plugging their talent gap.

4. People are good and well-intentioned, but we are all biased.

We have tremendous depth and expertise in Search, Recommendation and Personalization, and we are applying it to people and jobs.

We realized that the power of AI and our expertise in applying it at scale to the talent crisis should empower the job creators and job seekers to get better alignment — and quickly.

Information about the best candidates often lies in several different places, unable to be combined. Meanwhile, people apply and reapply to the same company with no record of their previous interest. HR executives are plagued with hiring issues: job hopping, the gig economy, diversity struggles and more.

The system has been broken.

Until now.

WHY WE WROTE THIS BOOK

Our research has been focused on finding innovative solutions to some of these issues by identifying a holistic approach to the search for meaningful work, one that uses cutting-edge artificial intelligence and machine learning to transform the talent acquisition and talent retention process for good — now and in the future.

We wanted to harness modern technology to simplify the job search, both for the applicant and employer. By combining an AI-powered platform with the skills and personal touch of an experienced HR professional, looking for your next role can be easier than it has ever been.

AI can help bridge the talent gap by providing candidates and employers with forward-looking insights that reveal not only what someone has done, but also powerful data on what they are capable of doing. With this data, companies can find, engage, and motivate their best people to help them achieve personal and business success.

These may sound like lofty goals, but they are achievable today. AI and machine-learning technology are progressing at incredible speeds, and our ability to aggregate and analyze information more effectively is one of the keys to helping to solve the talent gap in our companies and in our country, especially when it comes to helping people find a job that's a much better match — and ideally, the best possible match.

It is difficult to hire people, but it's even harder to keep good people. The average employee tenure at top technology companies is less than a year and half. Nationally, the stay is only four years!

Attrition is a huge problem. A recent survey by Robert Half showed a 22 percent increase in job hopping among workers as compared to four years ago.[6] There's a desire — perhaps more than ever — to find meaningful work that fulfills and energizes us, and to find employers and colleagues who share our values and help us be our best selves.

♂

A recent survey by Robert Half showed a 22% increase in job-hopping among workers as compared to four years ago.

When employees no longer feel stimulated by their work, or feel they do not have opportunities for internal growth, they will seek employment elsewhere. Turnover is at an all-time high, yet companies are not doing anything to keep their talent. While big budgets are being put towards recruitment, employee retention is being largely ignored, which just exacerbates the talent crisis. If people do not find work that properly satisfies them, they move on. We aim to get it right the first time, and we're ready to share our best practices, thought leadership, and research on

---

[6] Robert Half Survey via NBC News article. Retrieved: https://www.nbcnews.com/better/business/job-hopping-rise-should-you-consider-switching-roles-make-more-ncna868641

where we're headed so we can create a happier, more engaged workforce here and now.

HOW THE MAGIC HAPPENS

Using AI, we're revolutionizing the way HR professionals and executives hire and promote talent. Our platform predicts the potential of a particular candidate and his or her ability to learn a new skill required on the job — seeing far beyond what he or she has done in the past.

That's where the magic happens.

We can take an ideal candidate for a business and find similar candidates. This highly-effective process is particularly critical for companies hiring talent at scale, because it helps HR professionals systematically and proactively identify the best candidates without bias, greatly increasing the number of candidates that might be considered by using sophisticated, personalized algorithms to fit a business' specific needs. That means a much more diverse pool of talented potential employees will be organized and vetted for openings now and in the future, saving time, money, and resources.

As diversity and inclusion efforts continue to be an important part of HR initiatives nationwide, AI can be a powerful tool that can help provide masked screening. The technology, when used correctly, will reveal which applicants who have the most relevant expertise and who are likely to be an advantageous fit for available positions within the company by correlating skills to mathematical algorithms, removing potential for human bias.

Some of our current clients, such as Conagra Foods Inc, Tata Communications, AdRoll, and DigitalOcean, are using our proprietary AI process (which complies with all Equal Employment Opportunity regulations) to create more diverse organizations with significant results. Studies have shown that effective diversity initiatives tend to improve business outcomes — including everything from more creativity to better relationships with customers.[7]

AI IS AN ALLY

AI is an essential tool in retaining and promoting a diverse workforce. While AI technologies focus on identifying a strong match between a role and candidates based on public and company-specific data, AI also helps create more efficient and fair opportunities for promotions. We are constantly working on collecting more data to make our AI smarter and to present results in the best, most understandable and actionable format.

By utilizing AI effectively in HR recruitment, diversity initiatives, and in employee retention, businesses can drive innovation. The insights gained from creating robust profiles of potential candidates, employees, and companies means that companies can make highly

---

[7] Chignell, Barry. CIPHR. Retrieved via the internet: https://www.ciphr.com/advice/5-reasons-diverse-workforce-matters/

beneficial conclusions when it comes to hiring and promotions more quickly and with less financial strain.

Companies can hire and train for long and successful careers — a far more exciting offer than just getting another job that allows an individual to keep doing what they have been doing for the last several years.

Not only is good talent integral to running a successful business, making bad or misinformed hiring decisions can be expensive. It costs at least $5,000 to fill an open position. You have to pay to advertise your job, have someone screen applications, research candidates, and interview people — all while paying for a temp! On average, it takes 58 days to fill an open position. And once you've finally hired someone you're happy with, it takes almost one year — between training, adjustments, ramp-up time — until both employer and employee are productive and happy with each other.

That's a lot of money — and a lot of time.

This is an incredibly exciting time for AI and HR. Nearly any challenge facing HR professionals today can be solved by having access to better data and improved insights into finding and retaining the most talented candidates and helping them to find the most meaningful work possible.

Used responsibly, AI technology has the ability to greatly reduce human bias in the recruitment and retention process, and most importantly, to create a happier, more diverse workforce — the backbone of a productive and progressive society.

WHO ARE WE?

My name is Ashutosh Garg, and I am the Chief Executive Officer and Cofounder of Eightfold.ai. Eightfold's patented artificial intelligence–based platform empowers enterprises to turn talent management into a competitive advantage.

I've worked in Silicon Valley for decades, researching and implementing machine learning technology. Previously, I worked at Google for more than four years (which is eons in Silicon Valley!), where I led search and personalization efforts, and did the same for IBM. In 2009, I founded Bloomreach, a leading vendor for Digital Experience Platforms, aiming to optimize businesses' online platforms to drive conversion.

It's no coincidence we're working on this revolution in Silicon Valley. The tech capital of the world — perhaps best known for its innovative companies and a few genius startup founders who only wear T-shirts — has some of the highest attrition rates in the country. On average, employees stay fewer than two years, compared to the already low 4.2 years nationally.

Throughout my career, I've witnessed this attrition firsthand. I realized something had to change. I decided to combine my knowledge of AI technology and experience building great teams to help people find meaningful work, and in turn reduce employee turnover. After meeting Varun Kacholia at Google, we decided to team up to create Eightfold.

Varun is one of the world's leaders when it comes to search, ranking, and machine-learning. He's passionate about how AI can be applied to everyday life and really have a positive impact on people's lives.

Kamal Ahluwalia, president at Eightfold, joins me in writing this book.

We wrote *What's Next For You* for HR executives, C-suite executives, business owners, and job candidates. This book is for anyone and everyone who has hired or been hired by someone. We invite anyone concerned about the talent crisis to get engaged now in the solution. Indeed, you're a vital part of our next steps forward.

FINDING OUR POTENTIAL

At Eightfold, we talk a lot about meaningful employment for everyone. We are talking about billions of jobs, billions of skills, billions of job titles, millions of career options, multiple geographies, industries, and languages.

This is a problem worth solving that cannot be solved by individuals doing this manually or with archaic tools. It's a problem that is set up perfectly for AI and machine learning — because there's tons of data available about people, jobs, who companies do and don't like to hire, and an employee's own career trajectory, aspirations, competency and equivalency of skills, not to mention team environments where people tend to do well and those that could benefit from change. We have developed purpose-built models that enable us to make sense out of all this complex data and apply it to individual companies.

While we talk a lot about matching people to jobs, the accuracy of these recommendations and being able to explain the results is the key to building confidence among HR leaders and candidates. Today, we can provide this transparency to both. And we can make a recommendation specific to a person.

What is personally exciting for me and my team is to see how this can be applied to solve diversity and inclusion in our workforce. Yes, more and more CEOs genuinely care about diversity — and holding their teams accountable for it — and our platform can help them.

Most books written by entrepreneurs are after the fact. They have built a successful company and are now ready to share their learnings with others.

We want to encourage people to think differently about their talent problems right now. This change cannot and should not wait while Eightfold grows. We want more CEOs and CHROs to step back and rethink their talent strategy today. We know scale, because our past products are used everyday by billions of people worldwide.

HOW TO READ THIS BOOK

We've written this book to help you and your company be a part of the exciting transformation of talent acquisition and management happening right now. One by one, technology has revolutionized every industry. It started with transport during the industrial revolution, right to e-commerce with the rise of the internet. Up until now, hiring has remained largely untouched. Yes, computers and access to the internet have helped to simplify the application process for some, but the way we hire has remained stagnant for decades.

What we've discovered by creating Eightfold changes everything.

We want you to be a part of that change.

This book is here to guide you through how we are revolutionizing human resources for good. Join us.

Chapter 1

People Are Our Biggest Assets

"The secret of my success is that we have gone to exceptional lengths to hire the best people in the world."

Steve Jobs

ASSESSING THE PROBLEM

Companies around the globe currently face a skilled worker crisis.

Hiring managers fight hard to recruit skilled workers — often spending four to six months poring over resumes and interviewing potential candidates — but all too often, far too many still feel as though they can't find top talent. Ending up with less-than-desirable or downright bad hires can be expensive, and the lack of qualified workers results in the loss of productivity.

With such a lengthy recruiting process, and so little to show for it, it's clear the system is broken.

We all know that our people are our biggest asset — so why aren't we treating the system that finds, manages, and promotes them with more care and diligence?

From the United States, to India and the United Kingdom, there is a general consensus among employers that they are simply not finding the workers they need. Either there aren't enough skilled employees who possess the expertise to succeed in certain positions, or they're slipping through the cracks during recruitment. The millennial generation joining — and quickly taking over — the majority of the workforce is also contributing to this divide at some level as they bring different approaches and expectations to work than previous generations.

"Fundamentally, one of the most challenging things today is finding, retaining, motivating, developing, and growing talent, especially in the tech space," said Don Robertson, the Chief Human Resources Officer at Northwestern Mutual. "There is a tremendous gap in the capability of talent. And everybody's looking for the same talent, especially if you're geographically in a similar area."

That squeeze is being felt even by some of the world's most competitive and successful companies. In late 2018, Amazon announced it would build a new office in Washington, D.C. The company is investing $2.5 billion in the area, creating 25,000 new jobs at the new "headquarters" location. Not only will the move allow for the employment of 25,000 new Amazonians, but it will have a huge impact on the economy of the community, creating countless new jobs and spin-off businesses to serve the new employees. The Virginia Chamber Foundation expects the DC move to have a combined direct and indirect economic impact of $14.2 billion in Virginia, where the DC headquarters will actually be located, and by 2030 will support 59,308 jobs, when it reaches its full capacity.[8]

It's a sign of the times, but it's also a grave reminder for companies of all sizes in various industries to seek ways to "Amazon"-proof their organizations now, said Peter Nieh, founding partner at Lightspeed Venture Partners. For him, that means hiring for innovation.

"If you're General Electric, or you're State Farm Insurance, or you're Capital One, or you're Boeing, executives at

---

[8] Virginia Chamber Foundation. (2018). *Economic Impact of Amazon's Major Corporate Headquarters*. Richmond, VA: Chmura Economics & Analytics

these companies are running scared now seeing that technology could disrupt them and their businesses could dramatically fall in value if they're disrupted. So these companies are fiercely trying to hire technology innovation talent," he said. "What Eightfold represents is a competitive weapon for them to identify and hopefully attract the type of talent that they're going to need as they go through the next few decades of technology transformation of any business. None of them want to get Amazoned."

&

"What Eightfold represents is a competitive weapon to identify and attract the type of talent you're going to need as you go through the next few decades of technology transformation of any business."
— Peter Nieh, Founding Partner at Lightspeed Venture Partners

And while it might be easy to lay the blame on the current labor pool for lacking necessary skills to help mitigate this gap in talent, the discontent employees feel at their current workplaces points to a system deeply flawed on both sides. We'll go into more detail on this by presenting key data points from the recent Harris poll we conducted with employees and C-suite executives across the U.S. in later chapters.

Of course, the problem isn't just happening here in the United States. Numerous countries are experiencing rising turnover and attrition rates, causing industries to have decreased efficiency. It's clear change is needed. Now.

Research by The Open University in 2017 showed that 90 percent of employers in the U.K. struggled to recruit workers with adequate skills. The survey, which pulled data from 950 senior business leaders, also revealed that this shortage was costing businesses more than £2 billion a year in higher salaries, recruitment costs, and temporary staffing.

In 2018, Americans were quitting their jobs at such a rapid pace that it resulted in the highest quits rate since 2001. The U.S. Labor Department reported that the number of workers voluntarily leaving their jobs totaled 3.5 million as of December. The Job Openings and Labor Turnover Survey, or JOLTS, completed by the Labor Department also revealed there were 7.3 million unfilled jobs at the end of 2018, which shows how massive the shortage of skilled workers is countrywide.[9]

India is also struggling to fill positions and recruit skilled candidates. And once a position is filled, there's a good chance the employee will decide to leave shortly after.

"Studies show 75 to 90 percent of new employees will decide whether or not to stay in the job within the first six months of employment. Although high turnover costs may not produce recordable associated losses, many employers and HR professionals underestimate the high impact of hidden costs," said Mettl CEO and co-founder

---

[9] https://www.bls.gov/news.release/jolts.nr0.htm

Ketan Kapoor in an interview with The Hindu Business Line.

— ∞ —

Studies show 75-90% of new employees decide whether or not to stay in a job within the first 6 months

These turnover costs can run as high as $30,000 per lost employee, according to a study by Mercer Inc., an alarming figure when considering the rising turnover rates companies face.

But that cost is even *more* for highly skilled employees.

Plus, studies show it takes about one year to recover from the loss of a good employee in addition to the replacement cost.

Like the United Kingdom and the United States, India is also finding that there simply aren't enough skilled workers to go around. When companies do happen to find a skilled worker, they may feel compelled to offer a higher, competitive salary. This could add up to spending millions of additional dollars per year as a company grows and tries to compete.

And sadly, the employee churn rate is still very high — especially in coveted technical roles.

The Open University study found that, of the 950 businesses surveyed in the U.K., two thirds of employers felt obligated to increase pay, and 64 percent reported spending an additional £1.2 billion on recruitment. This level of loss provides a large incentive for companies to get serious about talent management, and to be proactive in implementing solutions.

The mismanagement of talent acquisition, lack of accountability, and the low priority of diversity all contribute to the troubling state of talent today.

In India, education is contributing to the country's challenge. The 2017 India Economic Survey by the Organization of Economic Cooperation and Development reported that public spending in India is 3.8 percent lower than countries such as Brazil and Malaysia. Students aren't being taught the technological skills needed to keep up with fast-changing business needs.

Mettl's recent Campus Hiring Report found that graduates of Indian Institutes of Technology and Indian Institutes of Management received 137 percent and 121 percent higher salary packages, respectively. Employers increasingly rely on recruiting from technical institutes because these students are among the few that possess the knowledge and practical skills to keep up with changing industries. In response, the Indian government is implementing several programs, like the Vocational Training Institutes for Women and Basic Training Centers, that encourage participants to develop the practical skills required for career success.

But what if we looked inside first? Helping current employees cultivate the knowledge necessary to succeed is another way employers can help to remedy the skilled worker shortage.

Lizzie Crowley, skills advisor at the Chartered Institute of Personnel and Development (CIPD) in the U.K., views this strategy as vital to accessing talent in a tight labor market.

"Now, more than ever, businesses must shift from a 'buy' to a 'build' strategy," she wrote in the 2018 report. "U.K. employers invest less than many other EU nations in training and developing their staff. With an ageing workforce, alongside the potentially reduced access to migrants in the future, it is critical that businesses focus on building the skills of their existing workforce."

We'll dive deeper into the evolving half-life of skills in a later chapter, as employees and managers all over the globe struggle to keep up.

A MORE HOLISTIC APPROACH

Clearly, competent employees that not only possess a required skill set, but who also match a company's values and culture are vital to the success of any business, big or small — so what can we do to create a space for talent to meet us halfway on either front?

As the gap between dissatisfied employers and unhappy employees continues to grow, so does the potential for widespread loss of productivity and financial resources. High turnover is also linked to reduced employee morale, lost company knowledge, and lost credibility in the marketplace.

While countries are slowly responding to changing needs in education, that is only one piece of the equation. To truly shift the efficiency of finding and retaining talent, companies need to identify holes in the recruiting process and implement new strategies. Traditional recruiting strategies often rely on incomplete data without providing a holistic glimpse at an individual's experience and skillset. It can turn into a game of profile analysis across isolated tools and agencies, which businesses have found increasingly ineffective.

All too often, many companies find themselves simply drowning in data.

Tech giant Microsoft provides one example of executives taking progressive action to overhaul an outdated HR system. Microsoft Chief Human Resources Officer Kathleen Hogan said in a recent interview with Gallup that the company decided to completely shift how the Human Resources Department looked for talent that would fill both current and future needs of the company.

"In the past we had a process called 'People Review' that ended up creating significant nervous energy for a lot of people," she said. "While the initial approach was sound, it had deteriorated into a process of number analysis, and wasn't yielding results. Our former CEO Steve Ballmer decided it wasn't adding value, and it was shuttered in 2014."[10]

Since the death of People Review, Microsoft has implemented a more thorough talent management system that includes expanding the pipeline of potential talent, and actively working to empower, mentor, and retain current employees. This is a vital shift for the company in terms of reducing turnover rates and costs, and one that other businesses struggle to mirror.

Glen Cathey, the senior vice president of global digital strategy at Randstad, also views traditional recruiting methods as somewhat limited. Cathey, who has more than 20 years of experience in recruiting and now focuses on innovation and the central application of AI, says there are two traditional paths of sourcing talent, one passive and one active.

---

[10] https://www.gallup.com/workplace/237113/microsoft-chro-conversation-succession-management.aspx

The passive approach consists of using employer branding and posting jobs, hoping the right people will stumble upon them and apply. This is a limited strategy, he says, as is the proactive approach companies have historically taken, which relies heavily on running keyword searches on the internet and on databases, which can only get a recruiter so far.

"You also have the intrinsic limitation of the data that you're actually searching," Cathey said. "When you're thinking about resumes and databases, or perhaps LinkedIn profiles, many of which are not fully filled out like a resume would be, you have less text to search and you have an even poorer insight into the people that you're trying to find. In some cases, you can't even find them because they don't say the words you're searching for."

Along with ineffective methods of sourcing talent, traditional talent management systems also tend to fall short when it comes to retaining people and understanding why employees choose to leave. Inadequate pay, poor work-life balance, and lack of professional development all influence to the decision to leave a position, according to research.

Companies may find it helpful to take a closer look at treatment and promotion of current employees, as well as what is contributing to the rapid loss of talent. Additionally, businesses must take the time to understand why employees are dissatisfied and how that can be remedied. In the case of Microsoft, implementing a new talent recruiting and management process helped address some of these issues.

"We take a look at talent that came into the group, and talent that went out, to see if we can identify patterns to understand why people are moving," Hogan said of the changes the HR team at Microsoft has implemented. "It's helpful to understand if the moves are simply career progression or something else so we can course-correct in areas that need help. We ask them to discuss how they're activating our culture, including being intentional about creating a diverse and inclusive work environment."

Microsoft upleveled its accountability of employee satisfaction, to the benefit of both talent and industry. But how can we all do this at scale in a cost-effective and efficient manner?

Increasingly, the answer is to utilize tools that make pattern-recognition easier — automating processes that can be automated, and eliminating human bias as much as, well, humanly possible by implementing tools such as masked screening. We'll go into these solutions in further detail in the chapters to come.

THE VALUE OF LOYALTY

Companies devote months to recruiting and wading through massive amounts of data, fighting to discover and keep skilled employees. Somehow, they still find themselves losing top talent, and the expensive process starts over.

In a study conducted with Harris Interactive Research in 2018, Eightfold found that 56% of job candidates have changed employers in the last 3 years and 84% are looking for a new position either with another company or with their current employer.

Evolving needs in the workplace that companies aren't addressing can help explain this turnover. This movement is partially due to the millennial generation entering the labor force, and bringing different values to company culture, and the increasingly common trend of job hopping rather than staying with a company for five to ten years.

That means, for better or worse, our younger colleagues are actually doing us a solid by showing us the error of our ways — and now we have the opportunity to fix it and take our recruitment and management efforts to the next level.

"The difference between today and 10 to 20 years ago is that it was frowned upon for people to change jobs on a frequent basis," Northwestern Mutual's CHRO Robertson added. "When I first came out of school, it was, 'why did you change jobs?' If you didn't stay in a job at least five to 10 years, people would look at you differently, and it was something as a candidate you'd have to overcome."

This poses another challenge for companies. If they don't treat their employees well, pay decent salaries, and provide work experiences to help them develop new skills, then it's highly likely another company will — or at the very least, another company will make such promises when trying to convince talent to join their team instead.

To improve employee retention, and satisfaction, employers can work to increase their level of accountability. Yes, we *know* people are every company's greatest asset, but there is an obvious disconnect when high numbers of employees feel undervalued, and quit as a result.

Feeling unappreciated can manifest in a multitude of ways. While one employee may feel as though they aren't given enough experiences to grow in the company, another may find their salary inadequate. Understanding this, and taking accountability for the situation, can improve the turnover rate.

But how can a CHRO or others on the executive team possibly keep up on the accomplishments of every employee, or connect them to ongoing opportunities for advancement or new challenges?

"Often companies, historically, have taken their current talent for granted, and are really focusing most of their energies on acquiring talent," said Robertson, "Which is often a big mistake, because you may already have a lot of really valuable talent, you just don't necessarily know it."

It is this recurring theme of ignoring — or at least not nurturing —current talent that allows competitors to recruit them, or for individuals to decide it's worth taking the risk of joining a new company, adjusting to a new supervisor and environment, and having to prove yourself again.

In addition, workers usually receive the best wage bump when they change jobs, according to senior economist Sophia Koropeckyj[11], which can make the move — and potential risk — worthwhile. Again, flaws in talent management systems contribute to this sense of neglect. In fact, the quits rates for American employees hit an all-time high in May 2018 — the highest it had been since 2001, according to the Labor Department.

Specifically, the lack of recruiting from inside the company and not assessing the current talent pool leads to employees feeling undervalued and stagnant at work.

Currently, without the use of AI, there is no sophisticated system for gathering data and assessing the talent pool already working inside a company. Employers tend to search solely outside of their company when a vacant position needs to be filled, which is clearly not always the most effective route. Providing the opportunity for a current employee to try out a new role, and gain new experience within the company, can build leadership skills and also result in increased productivity.

In fact, Hogan, and current Microsoft CEO Satya Nadella, held a number of roles in the company before settling into their current positions. This diverse set of experiences allowed them both to learn more about the organization, and more about how their specific skill sets could be most beneficial to Microsoft. Hiring from inside the company also means employees will bring some base knowledge of the organization into the new role,

---

[11] https://www.payscale.com/career-news/2018/08/quit-rate-heres-why-you-might-quit-your-job-soon

as opposed to an outside hire who has to spend months building that knowledge from the ground up.

THE NEW WORKFORCE

Millennials entering into the workforce also highlight the deep necessity of changing talent management techniques (as well as management and leadership techniques in general), as this group may be even more sensitive to stagnant roles than previous generations.

As a whole, younger workers aren't satisfied with silently sitting behind their desks and plugging away with the hopes of one day being promoted. Millennials are more keen to make an impact at work, more likely to ignore organizational boundaries, and increasingly content with quickly switching jobs if they feel the company culture is not meeting their needs.

For workers in the 25 to 35 age bracket, company culture matters so much that they would be willing to forfeit $7,600 of pay in exchange for more meaningful work or a better workplace fit, according to 2016 study by Fidelity Investments.[12] In fact, 58% of the millennials who responded said they would prioritize an improved "quality of work life" over financial benefits.

By 2020, millennials will comprise nearly half of the working population in the United States. Within the next three to four years, India will have the largest millennial

_____

[12] https://www.fidelity.com/about-fidelity/individual-investing/better-quality-of-work-life-is-worth-pay-cut-for-millennials

population in the world. In order to slow the rapid loss of talent, employers must adapt to these changing attitudes, as well as analyze how the recruiting process can attract better culture fits.

Recruiting from within the company may present another solution to millennial satisfaction and talent retainment. If a vacant role inside the organization provides a new challenge, and better leadership opportunities, these workers may be less likely to be lured away by competitors' promises of increased pay and responsibility. Millennial or not, one thing is certain: ignoring talent doesn't work anymore.

Lack of diversity in the office cannot be ignored any longer, either. Employees more often cite diversity and inclusion as important elements when considering a job offer. And if one organization doesn't meet their diversity requirements, another likely will.

Recently, there has been increased demand for gender equality in a number of industries, from tech to media and education, but this demand for inclusion extends to race, religion, sexual orientation, and mental and physical conditions. Millennials are helping to drive this trend, too.

In 2016, The Institute for Public Relations surveyed 1,000 U.S. adults and found that 47 percent of all millennials surveyed look for diversity and inclusion when assessing a potential job.

Equal pay also plays a key role in creating diverse, inclusive work environments, and making employees feel valued. If a woman or person of color discovers they're making less than a man in the same position, the chance they search for a higher-paying job, or become less productive, only increases. The outrage and push for change echoes in the public sphere, and is circulated in newspapers, magazines, and social media.

In 2018, it seemed more high-profile celebrities and professionals started speaking out and supporting the cause than ever before.

Late last year, NBA basketball star Stephen Curry penned a powerful blog post addressing the need for equal pay and equal opportunity. Thanks to the Sony hack a few years ago, Jennifer Lawrence discovered she was paid less than her male co-stars in the critically-acclaimed film, "American Hustle."

Fellow award-winning actresses Natalie Portman, Taraji P. Henson, and Emma Stone all spoke about the reality of earning less than their male counterparts, despite equal amounts of screen time. Stone even revealed some of her male co-stars have taken pay cuts so that she can have parity with them.

Far from being contained to American film stars, the pay gap is just as prevalent in Europe. Almost three quarters of companies in the U.K. pay men more than they pay women, according to Government Equalities Office data. And the BBC reported that the Bank of

England's wage rate for men is 24 percent higher than for its female employees.

Not only is there a moral case for employers to respond to this call, there is a business case as well. Crafting a diverse workforce means employees with a wide array of industry experiences, worldviews, and thought processes are brought together, and can then utilize these differences for faster, more innovative products and solutions.

Research done by Deloitte shows that diversity of thinking leads to enhanced creativity and productivity. On average, it takes input from six different mental frameworks to solve a complex problem, the report says. Since no individual is equally competent at all six, complementary colleagues need to fill the knowledge gaps. Diversity in a group helps elicit cognitive diversity and innovation. Inclusion helps ensure those diverse perspectives contribute to the best possible solutions for people, products, and companies.

People matter, and all people should have an equal opportunity to have success in meaningful careers. Lack of inclusivity is another form of ignoring talent, and evidence of poor talent management. If each employee feels valued, morale and loyalty will only grow within the company.

PEOPLE FIRST, AI SECOND

Enhanced recruiting techniques that incorporate masked screening or other sophisticated AI tools may help rid hiring managers of unconscious bias as much as possible, and provide a more comprehensive analysis of incoming resumes when executives just don't have the time to pore through them. In addition, comprehensive job matching made possible by machine learning can help internal candidates find the next opportunity quickly and easily.

That's critical in today's hyper-competitive, talent-strapped economy.

Eightfold's Director of Event and Field Marketing Cherrie McKinnon can attest to the reality of these issues from a hiring perspective and the importance of utilizing an AI solution.

"You just don't have time to review all the resumes that are coming your way," she said. "So for me, this was a real-life issue that I've dealt with in the past: for example, I need to hire three field marketing people in the next few months, and I just don't have time because I'm trying to keep up with my everyday work. So you sit with a recruiter for a few minutes a week, and they're feeding you resumes, and they don't necessarily know what you need."

So how many companies across the globe are coping with the exact same problem as we speak? When we're assessing these issues on an even larger scale, it's clear why change is needed to ensure the best hires are reachable not only now, but as your organization continues to grow.

"But just in my business, if I've hired more than 6,000 people globally, this is across 20 different locations in more than 10 countries. You can imagine how difficult it is to keep quality, keep true to quality and true to what what you're looking for when you're dealing with people who are fitting into a matrix organization across the world," Rajeev Butani, the senior managing director at Accenture, a global management consulting firm, said.

So how can we better address such a multi-faceted issue and, at the same time, avoid such a rapid loss of talent?

The key lies in balancing the act of effective talent acquisition, while recruiting diverse employees, and also empowering current employees to grow. Seems simple enough, right? Most importantly, any solution to these issues must include a strategy for dealing with growth and application at scale.

"The challenge that I've seen all through my life, whenever you start to deal with scale from a hiring perspective, is you tend to compromise on quality," Butani added. "You tend to make your process less intelligent and less effective."

As part of the six-person team that launched Accenture's global delivery network, Butani saw firsthand how important recruiting the right team was for the company's success. To him, "it's all about finding the right talent. It's all about creating the right capability."

Utilizing AI in the talent management sphere ensures that quality isn't compromised when hiring managers get too busy, or the process turns into a never-ending numbers game. There has been proven success among companies that have tested AI technologies for talent management purposes.

Nick Mailey, vice president of Talent Acquisition at Intuit, applied AI technology to talent acquisition and found that the system helped weed out the unqualified applicants so they could reach the 10 percent of applicants who were qualified.

In a recent podcast interview, Mailey said the system "reviewed about 6,000 resumes, and basically suggested that they weren't matches for the kinds of talent we were looking for. It was, I think, 90 percent of the applicants that applied were not qualified for our technical roles."

Above all, the most promising finding of Mailey's experience was the increased speed of hire. The team found they shaved nine days off the recruiting process, and there was a 48-point lift in NPS. At large companies that receive massive numbers of resumes, this type of system is much more effective than relying solely on recruiters to skim through and pick out applicants, many of whom won't be a great match in the first place.

Through creating a comprehensive talent network, personalizing the recruiting process, and utilizing artificial intelligence to streamline data, Eightfold.ai is working to solve the talent crisis affecting companies today. Our proprietary, purpose-built Talent Intelligence

Platform helps employers find qualified candidates through AI-based ranking, which looks at applicants holistically, rather than relying on keyword matches.

By utilizing this AI technology, companies can also work on providing current employees further opportunities for growth, and start inside recruiting. Since the platform holds data on all past, current, and potential employees, the process of analyzing talent matches and offering lateral transfers within the company becomes much simpler.

Artificial intelligence can also strip unconscious bias from the recruiting process in creative ways, thus promoting diversity and inclusion for all potential hires. One clever feature in the Eightfold.ai platform is the removal of names and photos from the applications, which is also known as masked screening.

This is a game-changer, according to case studies and experts in the field.

"If you can see someone's name, you can, more often than not, immediately know a number of things about them, and it's all unconscious," said Randstad's Cathey. "With some exceptions, you often gain insight into the person's gender. Some names provide clues into race, and you can sometimes tell what their ethnicity might be. With other information commonly found on resumes, you may also be able to tell if they went to school outside the U.S., if they're an immigrant and come from another country, or if they are over 40 years of age. And It would be foolish to think that people don't have some degree of unconscious bias going on when reviewing resumes and profiles. As such, every company should investigate the options available for using technology to try to mitigate that unconscious bias."

Whether it's matching qualified candidates, developing current talent, or promoting diverse work cultures, AI technology has proven to enhance talent management through all steps of the process. People are any the greatest asset of any business, and we can no longer afford to ignore or lose them.

It's time to put more humanity back into the talent recruiting and management process.

TOP TALENT TIPS

1. Review your current talent pipeline with your executive team: where do you see gaps or areas of opportunity?

2. Consider recent data on attrition and assess whether or not you have enough qualified talent lined up internally or externally to jump in at a moment's notice.

3. Review your current diversity numbers across current employees and outside candidates, and assess how many currently deployed diversity candidates could be capable for open roles based on experience.

Chapter 2

The Impact Of Talent Management Done Right

&

"The most fundamental and important truths at the heart of Extreme Ownership: there are no bad teams, only bad leaders."

Jocko Willink, Extreme Ownership: How U.S. Navy SEALs Lead and Win

MAKING THE BUSINESS CASE FOR CHANGE

"If you win the war for talent, you win the business war," said Aubrey Blanche, global head of diversity & belonging at Atlassian. "Every company is hiring at higher volume, at higher scale. The only way to cope with that change and keep your talent bar high is to do it through some kind of technological augmentation."

Successful talent management may not be an easy feat — but the innovations in AI and machine learning are making it possible for all of us to do it well.

And if you don't? There are real, tangible effects of poor hiring practices, retention rates and training. If your company doesn't do talent management well, it *will* cost you time and money.

———————— ∂ ————————

"If you win the war for talent, you win the business war."
— Aubrey Blanche, Global Head of Diversity & Belonging at Atlassian

Unfilled positions mean that work isn't getting done. If you can't find the talent necessary to run your business you lose money.

As of the end of 2018, there were more than 7.3 million open jobs in the United States, according to a U.S.

Bureau of Labor statistics report. In 2017, Glassdoor estimated the value of unfilled advertised jobs was more that $272 billion[13].

There are more than 7 million open jobs in the United States

So you're not alone — but is a trouble shared really a trouble halved?

Partnering with Harris Media, we conducted more than 1,200 interviews during the summer of 2018. We learned that companies can't hire fast enough to grow and backfill for attrition, leading to lost growth. Diversity programs are failing, and most employees want to change roles.

---

[13] https://www.glassdoor.com/press/glassdoor-introduces-salary-estimates-job-listings-reveals-unfilled-jobs-272-billion/

An incredible 28 percent of open roles will not be filled in the next 12 months and almost half of top talent will quit within two years, according to the survey. Clearly, we are all doing something wrong — or as we might say in Silicon Valley: this is an opportunity for disruption.

But we need to act quickly.

Two-thirds of CEOs and CHROs interviewed admitted that they find it difficult to retain their talent, while 73 percent agreed that finding talent is a key issue.

We're in one of the tightest labor markets in recent history, as the U.S. economy is experiencing the lowest unemployment rate in 30 years. Because of this tightness in the supply chain of employees, the cost of running talent acquisition initiatives has risen hugely in the last few years. People can jump around from job to job, and in doing so can leave you with not only a huge gap to fill, but a large invoice to boot.

Things are so tight that if you lose a key engineer in the middle of an important project, you could put the company behind for six months while you find and train someone to replace them — just because of one employee leaving!

But it's not just financial capital that you might be losing. Spreading your employees too thin means you could lose them to overwork and fatigue, too. Not only does the 28 percent of jobs unfilled hurt your top line, it means more work for your employees that stay.

As they continue their own tasks, the rest of the work from unfilled positions must still get done — and often without acknowledgment or a pay increase. Undoubtedly, this will eventually lead to job dissatisfaction or worse. It will affect their emotions and feelings about your company, and before you know it, you could lose them, too.

It goes without saying that when morale is low, work quality and productivity — to say nothing of innovation and creativity — suffer.

It's *bad* news to have unfilled jobs. Still, you can't afford to make a bad hire, no matter what.

If you think leaving a position open is negative, let's think about the consequences of making a bad hire and the costs associated with replacing those who leave without a succession plan in place.

For highly-skilled employees, the cost of replacement can be astronomical, with one of the Center for American Progress[14] estimating that losing executive-level employees could cost up to 213 percent of their annual salaries.[15]

If one of your top employees — who was being paid, say, $100,000 — leaves you in the lurch, you could be out $213,000. That's tough to swallow.

---

[14] https://www.americanprogress.org/wp-content/uploads/2012/11/CostofTurnover.pdf

[15] https://www.americanprogress.org/issues/economy/reports/2012/11/16/44464/there-are-significant-business-costs-to-replacing-employees/

Losing executive-level employees could cost up to 213% of their annual salaries

Not only does the loss of your top talent cost you, but making the wrong decision afterward also means investing in onboarding, salary, sign-on bonuses, and benefits for a new employee who potentially cannot or won't do the job to the standards required — or one who is likely to leave after only a few months.

What's the cost of that bad hire staying on? Not only does poor performance bring down your top line, additional costs can extend to exit interviews, accrued vacation time and other separation costs and, in some cases, legal fees. Not to mention the overtime pay that might be necessary for other employees who have to make up the work, and other productivity-related costs, such as paying for a temporary worker or interim executive.

Ultimately, you're back where you started: spending even more on advertising, pre-screening, interviewing, doing background checks and other hiring related costs.

Bad hiring is *expensive*.

A NEW WAY OF THINKING

So what can be done? Change needs to come from the top, and many CEOs and CHROs recognize there is a problem in the way we've been approaching talent management. Fifty-nine percent of those interviewed say that creating a better experience for internal and external candidates is important — and 64 percent believe increasing talent retention is important, according to the Harris Media Survey.

It's up to the management to change the talent management culture of a company. One solution is to create dedicated teams that simplify processes for employees in the hopes of increasing retention.

Monika Fahlbusch is an experienced HR executive, currently with Juul Labs. She helped Salesforce grow from a few thousand to 17,000 employees. As Chief Employee Officer at BMC Software, she was charged with making sure everything employees experience was as easy as possible so they could stay focused on being productive, innovative, and ultimately happy team members.

"Our team was responsible from everything having to do with onboarding, IT provisioning, hiring, performance management, real estate, facilities management, security, travel and all communications," she said. "We felt that we could shield employees from all the 'sausage-making' and all the different processes — we wanted to make it a different engagement and pull it all together."

By creating a dedicated team that aimed to simplify processes for employees, BMC showed they care about their employees and are dedicated to their success. Although the program hasn't been running long enough to have robust quantitative results, BMC has introduced metrics to hold these processes accountable.

It represents a huge shift in thinking about how we think about the notion of managing talent — and how we measure our impact in doing so successfully.

"Eightfold is doing something that is noble in my view, and the reason why it's noble is because the way we talk about reducing waste, and the way we talk about going green, I consider this going green inside a company," said Rajeev Butani, senior managing director at Accenture. "Because if you don't have the right people, and if they're not working with the right level of their aptitude and capacity, there is a significant amount of waste that goes on."

As for BMC, diminishing that sort of "waste" is becoming a part of the cultural fabric of the HR organization.

"So far, the early reads are that it completely has changed the mindset of everybody who works in employee experience, because they know that they're accountable to those metrics and those measures," said Fahlbusch.

No matter how you choose to run the talent management side of your business, it's critical that it is in line with your overall business *and* organizational strategy. For Russell Williams, a global HR executive and the President & Founder of HR Global Link, that means putting people first.

"Business strategy addresses profit and product and all those kinds of things, but the organizational strategy addresses the people component of that equation," he said. "And both of those two strategic components need to be aligned."

EMPOWERING EXECS TO MAKE THE LEAP

So how can we think about reframing how motivation and retention of top talent ties into an organization's structure, and further into a company's strategic goals?

Perhaps the secret to successful talent management is empowerment of the leaders who can say yes to making a leap towards the future now. They say the first step to solving any problem is acceptance — and that is true in this situation, too. Leaders need to have the confidence to admit the current talent management system is outdated and broken. By saying you are ready to make a change, that you feel empowered to be a part of the solution, you are already on the right track because you're open to making changes.

Any change has to come from the top.

But it's also about empowering your employees. Offering programs that make them feel valued is integral in keeping them at your organization, because here's the thing: a lot of employees don't *want* to leave your organization, they just want a better environment, acknowledgment of their accomplishments, and — definitely — new challenges.

The 2018 Eightfold Harris Media study revealed that 83 percent of employees want a new job. Only 53 percent want to change companies.

The 2018 Eightfold Talent Intelligence & Management Report revealed that 83% of employees want a new job, but only 53% want to change companies.

Many admitted they would stay for fair compensation, better culture, better work relationships and more enjoyable work, among other things. As we've seen from the cost analysis at the beginning of the chapter, it's of course not only smart business, but more cost-effective to incentivize your employees to stay rather than try to find new ones over and over again.

Even doing something as simple as introducing referral programs can be a factor in incentivizing people to stay. Referral programs can be more than a lead source for your company. Typically, employees won't refer friends unless they are proud of their current employer. Plus, if people are surrounded by friends at work, they tend to become more emotionally invested, and therefore less likely to leave.

That makes employee referrals invaluable to any company. We know that most successful organizations trust the word of their employees, evidenced by the fact that 15 to 50 percent of new employees are hired via internal referrals. This channel is significant, because it doesn't help current employees if they're bringing in candidates who will negatively contribute to the company's success.

And while the cost of a bad hire is well understood, a bad referral can reflect just as poorly on the employee. It is in their interest, as well as the organization's, to bring high-quality candidates into the company. The cost of hire and time to hire is better for referrals, since it's clear the candidate being referred is already interested in joining your company. It's also one of the huge opportunities in solving for effective talent management right now through Eightfold's platform.

Sixty-four percent of CEOs and CHROs admit the inability to find different or better roles internally compels people to leave their organizations, according to our Harris Media Survey.

Rethinking talent management means thinking about career guidance— being proactive in helping your diverse team to thrive at every step in his or her career is just smart business.

But with hundreds or thousands of employees in your system in a large organization — who can keep track?

Believe it or not, AI can be a great empowerment tool.

With Eightfold, you can transform the employee experience. Let your valued team members self-select their career paths, explore options, find mentors, and talk to peers who have made similar decisions — at their convenience: weekends, evenings, whenever and wherever they choose.

This is what Amazon and Netflix have taught us. And AI can bring a similar experience to career planning.

When we talk about career planning, we aren't referring to just the next rung up on the same ladder. We're interested in probing what it means to have a meaningful career path: How do I become a Vice President? How do I have a career like my CEO? What do I need to learn? What am I missing? Will a specific class or seminar help me get to the next level? Or do I need first-hand experience in a role or a chance to do what I do know on a larger scale? How can I shape my career? Or how do I switch to a different career path or industry altogether? What does that look like? Who can I talk to? Am I capable of making the switch and having success? Who else has done so and can they help me?

AI can help reveal the answers to all of these questions and more, because we can map out multiple career paths with considerable accuracy. This is the experience that millennials and Gen-Z employees want. And this is the experience that Gen-X employees need — especially if they're interested in staying competitive by upskilling or reskilling. This is the experience necessary for all employees going forward — to feel informed and empowered. This is why we started Eightfold.

With AI, we can map out multiple career paths with considerable accuracy. This is the experience that millennials and Gen-Z employees want, and this is the experience that Gen-X employees need.

Fundamentally, Eightfold is built for internal mobility, because it can cater to every employee and candidate at scale. If you haven't checked in with an employee for a while, it can remind you. AI platforms like Eightfold can make sure that you also look for your *current* employees to fill any open positions. It helps you look after the employees you have, making them feel more valued and making sure they don't get passed up for promotions they deserve, implicitly helping to solve some of the most pressing diversity issues facing organizations today. (We'll cover bias in talent management more thoroughly in **Chapter 6: Bias Is a Four-Letter Word**.)

It can also give you and your employees the freedom to focus on higher-value tasks as the mundane becomes automated. Eightfold saves you time — literally from hours to days — in filtering candidates, performing background checks and comparing skill sets. It gives you, as the executive or hiring manager, extra time to manage and lead — rather than push paper.

And as any good leader knows, time is the one thing you can't replace.

"The keen executive takes that extra time and says, now I'm going to do fireside chats with my team," said James Kinney, director of people at Giant Spoon. "Now I'm going to sit face-to-face with someone instead of emailing them. Now I'm going to say: what can I do to support minorities in my workplace? What can I do to support women in the workplace? Let me look at my salaries and see: are there disparities between women and men and what they're paid in our workplace?"

It's bringing the human touch back to human resources, Kinney said: "You know, as oxymoronic as that may sound as an outsider, this technology gives us opportunities to actually be more human."

TOP TALENT TIPS

1. Want to know how much each unfilled job is costing you? To work out how much the average cost of each unfilled job, divide your total annual revenue by the number of people in your company. Then, divide this number by 365 to get your daily revenue per employee, and multiply it by the average number of days a position goes unfilled in your company. Finally, multiply this by the number of open positions you have and — voila, you can see just how much you're losing by letting jobs go unfilled.

2. Take the Eightfold Challenge: Let's pretend we're in the same room together. Think about where the potential opportunities lie within your own existing HR management systems. Our average client has 250 times the employees in a talent pool frozen in time. Consider assessing what changes could be made with that data within the next 60 days if you had an AI-based tool to help you organize and analyze it.

3. Review the average time spent on hiring and training new talent — talk with your department heads about areas of opportunity for better communication and accountability for the development of talent company-wide, whether it's through seminars, continuing education, or guest lectures.

Chapter 3

Your Talent Network

"Whether you believe you can or you believe you can't, you are right."

Henry Ford

Building and maintaining a comprehensive talent network is an essential step companies should take to not only simplify the recruiting process, but to stay competitive.

Access to an intelligent talent network comprised of applicants, current employees, and company alumni can streamline the talent acquisition process and provide more efficient job matches. Working on engaging with these networks, and tapping into underutilized talent, also gives an edge to attracting the top, skilled talent that almost all businesses are struggling to find in today's talent-strapped job marketplace.

Generally, a company with 10,000 employees will attract a talent pool of roughly two million candidates. Think about that for a moment. Two million resumes or profiles of people who have either expressed interest in, or who have in the past, worked for you. With such steep numbers, even the most successful HR team couldn't possibly have the time or resources to comb through each profile and analyze all the data to ensure the best candidate is matched to a certain role. Utilizing AI in this space will allow businesses to garner more control over their talent networks, more control over their hiring processes, and improved ability to leverage their brand equity.

ARE YOU IGNORING YOUR BRAND'S EQUITY WHEN YOU RECRUIT TALENT?

As a business expands and crafts a popular public brand, it's not unusual for more people to want to work with them. This greater awareness is, of course, a good thing — and typically manifests in more candidates — whether or not the company has actually leveraged its brand equity to help facilitate higher candidate interest or has the internal processes in place to handle the influx of interest.

As consumers and as employees, we want to work with brands that are easy to engage with, progressive, and able to provide great value and service. For example, Netflix and Amazon have made it easy for us to interact with them as consumers — priding themselves on great customer service and quality offerings available at our fingertips anywhere, anytime. With AI, companies can leverage this kind of equity and attract a stronger pool of talent that is genuinely invested in the company culture. When people know and like your company, taking advantage of brand equity is one giant step toward enhancing the number of quality candidates who will continue to build that brand loyalty on your behalf internally and externally.

Your employees can then become some of your greatest brand ambassadors.

Organizations like DigitalOcean have found success with systems that create a robust network of past applicants. These profiles are automatically updated through the software, so recruiters can quickly comb through qualified candidates they know are likely still interested in working for the company.

In the past, it wasn't as necessary to keep past applicants in mind. Now, in a competitive market, brands can't afford to ignore this talent pool when big companies like Amazon or Netflix could steal away the best of the best talent. It's a risk we just can't afford to take.

Massive, highly popular companies like Apple or Facebook will naturally bring in thousands of resumes simply because their products are popular, and their brands feel accessible. People want to work for them. They're invested in the brand's ethos — or at least their perception of it. When competing with such companies for top recruits, taking full advantage of your unique brand equity can help offset the advantage larger corporations earn just from their brand name.

Eightfold helps during this talent acquisition process by enhancing engagement and content development with precise recommendations. Using sophisticated data analysis, Eightfold can create personalized emails and events for applicants with the convenience and efficiency of automation through AI.

Personalization in communication efforts makes a company feel more accessible and likeable: hallmarks of businesses with high loyalty among customers and candidates alike. It makes the candidate feel important (as they should), and shows your company took the time to determine what is relevant to him or her specifically.

When the company is successful in proposing the next step in a candidate's career progression, they are hooked even before the first live conversation. The company and the brand feels more accessible and likeable.

This sense of nurturing candidates is a powerful tool in today's market, where employers need qualified candidates more than applicants need job openings. Instead of competing with gimmicky promises, tailoring interactions with interested applicants will prove more beneficial in the long run.

Even if an applicant isn't hired, they will recall the positive engagement, and possibly wish to reconnect with the company later on, or recommend it to a friend who might be a great fit as well.

When candidates feel as though a company is truly committed to assisting them in career growth, whether they're hired or not, that company's talent network will widen.

WHEN THE TRAIL STOPS WITH THE EXIT INTERVIEW

A strong, manageable talent network is even more vital now as job turnover rates and the cost of lost employees continue to rise. Harnessing the power of your alumni network is one way to leverage brand equity, while also fully utilizing the depth of your talent pool.

Historically, the methods and strategies involved in alumni management weren't as imperative to a company's success. People remained in one job for much longer, and dealing with things like exit interviews just wasn't a top priority.

The opposite is true of the modern workforce. Instead of resigning from a company two or three times in a career, modern workers may resign closer to 15 or 20 times.[16] When facing a shrinking skilled labor pool and high turnover rates, maintaining and engaging with alumni networks means improved access to top talent.

Handling exit strategies should be a core competency for any business. People are the greatest asset of any company, and that extends to company alumni.

Traditionally, the loss of an employee would have been dealt with by perhaps offering a hasty exit interview as a formality without much of an attempt to keep in touch.

What's worse, there hasn't been a convenient or useful way to keep in touch with lost talent, which is a missed opportunity companies can't afford to make any longer, says Kelly O. Kay, managing partner of the software and internet practice at Heidrick & Struggles, a retained executive search firm.

Kay says making the most of your company's alumni network to create an avenue for them to possibly return to the company can be invaluable.

"Nobody on the planet will have the exact same one by definition," Kay says. "Your alumni network is unique. So, to have that alumni network insight — what you

---

[16] Monika Hamori, Jie Cao, and Burak Koyuncu. "Why Top Young Managers Are in a Nonstop Job Hunt". *Harvard Business Review*. July-August 2012 Issue.

could do with it — could mean the difference between winning and losing, or being competitive or not."

Kay helps companies recruit on an executive level and believes alumni networks could be helpful in assessing past employees who have maintained, or improved, their skill-sets, and also in providing a chance for impressive talent to return. Even if company alums never come back, having a consistent channel of communication with them and knowledge about their career trajectories could greatly improve company culture.

When an employee leaves, there's always a chance that some company knowledge will not be transferred to the person new in the role. This could be a particular hindrance to businesses when the employee stepping down was a key player, one who contributed to integral programs or projects. James Kinney, director of people at Giant Spoon, says this type of knowledge is rarely recorded, so when the employee is gone, their projects walk out the door with them, too.

Developing an alumni network will help companies recover this lost knowledge, which will in turn strengthen the capabilities of new employees. Giving alumni opportunities to teach and pass on their experience also builds brand loyalty that will improve future talent recruiting. Kinney views proper employee exit strategies as critical to a company's future innovation, and not something to be quickly glossed over.

So what's at stake if you ignore your alumni and let them speak their minds with megaphones?

"If you do it the wrong way, you're going to get a two-star review on Glassdoor. And, you know, it's kind of like Yelp," he says. "Whether the person is crazy as hell, or they're right, people are still going to read the Glassdoor [review]. If you have two stars, it's going to affect your recruiting. So I would think that the alumni program is really important, and make it a coachable and teachable moment."

GETTING TIME BACK

The Eightfold Talent Intelligence Platform closes the gap between alumni and employers, and allows companies to continue building brand loyalty and engagement. Not only does the platform provide access to a comprehensive talent network containing all candidates, employees, and alumni, it also gives executives and hiring managers more time to focus on what matters most by automating data gathering functions.

"The most valuable commodity that any recruiting organization has is time," said Daniel Doody, head of EMEA recruitment at Zendesk.

Stanford University Professor Michael Ross agrees, especially when it comes to reframing the current approach to talent acquisition known as "closing the req" with a new one that might take longer, but ultimately will lead to better results.

"Someone who considers themselves successful might say, 'I closed 100 reqs and I did it in 6.7 days. Isn't that great?'" he said. "But, then they'll think: 'Wait a second — I want to have a more diverse organization.' Studies show that recruiting people who aren't similar to you takes longer. That's where AI can help."

Since AI is more efficient in gathering and analyzing data in the talent network, CHROs can instead take the time to focus on improving company culture and aligning their talent strategy with the overall company strategy, which recent research shows is critical.

This may mean increased face time with employees and managers, and developing solutions for issues of diversity and salary gaps in the company, all of which influence employee satisfaction levels — and ultimately, your company's bottom line.

But let's go back to the very beginning — a very good place to start, some might say.

AI helps open the channel between past and present employees, while also managing growing talent networks from day one. This data-driven talent management philosophy extends beyond the recruitment process to onboarding employees. The first few weeks and months in a role can set a new employee up for success or failure. Extending better network management to the onboarding process can provide a needed edge to retain top talent and cultivate company loyalty.

Growth strategist Kinney experienced the success of nontraditional onboarding while consulting for Hoff, a German HR talent platform. Hoff's onboarding module included 90 days of onboarding, which Kinney says can have a massive impact on employee retention and success.

"It sounds like a lot, but that's when you're setting the tone for the relationship," he says. "It's like dating. You know, that honeymoon period — how you do things together and how you overcome adversity is really important for the rest of your relationship. So let's reimagine onboarding. That's the cool thing that Eightfold does, too. You can see the onboarding journey."

Effective training and onboarding is increasingly paramount in modern talent networks. Technology and software is changing rapidly, to the point that certain skills can prove obsolete a year or two after acquiring them. More and more companies are feeling the strain of a skilled worker shortage. This poses a challenge not only to the employee, but to the employer, who may struggle to translate old skills into what capabilities are needed in an open position. (We'll cover this further in **Ch. 4 The Half-Life of Skills Is Shrinking Fast**.)

"Domain experience is a lot less important today, because every company in the world is transforming themselves," says Hendricks & Struggles' Kay. "If they're an industrial company, or a financial services company, or a consumer products company, they're using software in ways that they've never used software before, and they're probably becoming more software-like."

Kay noted that, on a global level, nearly all companies are becoming more software-like because they're using data like they've never used it before to understand the consumer and to modernize outdated or inefficient processes.

"Every company is going through this enormous transformation," he said.

Still, domain knowledge can be taught to new employees, and you already have hundreds of people well versed in the industry who are experts.

However, as you transform your business, it is smart to bring in new talent that is not burdened with past habits, and instead bring the new skills and capabilities that the company needs to complete and sustain the transformation — not to mention a refreshing new look on what's next for your company.

A CHANGING WORKFORCE

When interviewing, rather than focusing solely on what a candidate has done in the past, employers need to hire for potential. They should assess what an interested applicant could bring to the table, and who they could become in the company if given the right opportunity. Good onboarding techniques, and a sense of re-education upon starting a job, can offset the effects of a tight labor market by helping to build and retain a solid talent network. This strategy will help new talent feel included in the company culture early on, which the millennial workforce has proven to place greater stock in than previous generations.

The need for re-education and re-skilling extends to current company employees that are struggling to adapt to changing environments and values. As technology progresses and younger employees flood the workforce, this has become a particularly common issue.

The average person's knowledge base has a half life of about four and a half years, because the speed of technology is outperforming human capabilities.

This alarming expiration date, paired with the challenge executives and businesses face in managing the millennial talent network, points to the need for some level of re-education. Instead of placing the blame solely on employees, employers must work on building stronger leaders and nurturing skills to adapt. Studies point to millennials, above all, wanting engagement in their work and help developing their careers. Most importantly, every company needs to reward people who take the initiative to learn new skills that align with the company's strategy.

According to a 2016 report from Gallup, millennials are the least engaged in their jobs, with only 29 percent of participants reporting active engagement.[17] This is a big problem for a generation that desires more meaningful work and hands-on career development.

Lack of training, and lack of feeling as though their employers are committed to assisting with career growth, is why this group is more open to new

---

[17] 2016 Gallup Report: "How Millennials Want to Work and Live".

opportunities and job hopping. Organizations tend to use a trickle-down approach when it comes to training. More money is spent on senior leadership and less at the lower manager and employee levels. While it's understandable that companies may not want to make a large financial commitment to train new workers who could leave, having no plan for training new hires almost guarantees they will leave in search of the next best opportunity. Workers also increasingly wish to work with leaders who act more as coaches rather than bosses in the traditional sense.

Eightfold's Talent Intelligence Platform makes it easier to provide higher levels of engagement and personalization throughout the entire hiring and onboarding process, making it far simpler for companies to accommodate these changing values. Recruiters using Eightfold report 90 percent less time spent on sourcing, but report up to seven times higher response rates. That's the kind of ROI that can move the needle in terms of meeting your goals *and* create meaningful change for your employees.

AI technology provides greater insight into applicants, so as to improve and personalize the candidate experience, which recruiters will actually have the time to do when utilizing a streamlined talent network.

As mentioned earlier, this type of detailed attention only strengthens a company's talent network, and provides a needed competitive edge in a tight labor market. If candidates feel as though a company is truly committed to assisting with career growth, whether hired or not, that company's talent network continues to widen. Applicants will view that organization more positively, and want to work there, even if they aren't hired immediately.

A strong alumni network also ties into this idea of retraining employees, and ensuring new hires are given the skills and guidance they need to succeed in a position. Alumni can help pass on this knowledge, and bolster company culture. And a channel of communication with alumni signals to new employees that they will still be valued by the company if they do choose to leave, and that the organization truly is committed to assisting with career growth at all levels. If managed well, each element of a strong talent network leads to stronger brand loyalty which can then be leveraged to attract top talent.

Reinforcing diverse skill-sets makes it easier to retain a wide network, and avoid the high costs associated with losing employees. Ensuring employees have transferable skills helps with career growth, and diminishes the feeling that they are stuck in rigid roles with no room for change.

Eightfold Director of Event and Field Marketing Cherrie McKinnon speaks to the importance of fostering movement within a company, and how AI can help.

"Let's say I have only been doing events my whole career, and then I think I can only get a job in events," she says. "Whereas, I think the AI aspect of what we're doing is kind of saying, 'Cherrie you've been doing events and now your next progression could be this, this and this.'

So to me, that's super exciting because I don't think people really necessarily think that way. They think, 'it's really difficult to change careers. It's really difficult, you have to start over.'"

AI can help manage lateral movement in an organization, while retaining company loyalty, culture, and knowledge. Again, it reinforces that management is committed to assisting with career growth and keeping employees engaged. The Talent Intelligence Platform can analyze current employee data more efficiently and identify the various roles in which each person may excel. Instead of an employee thinking they must go to another company if they want to progress, or change, the trajectory of their career, AI technology helps find alternatives.

Kinney also views a sense of dynamism and transferable qualities as vital to a thriving company. Wearing just one mask or embodying just one role can ultimately make an organization or even a department or group stale. To Kinney, this is unsustainable.

"That's what I'm really big on: I want someone from, perhaps, the product team to give me their perspective on marketing," he said. "Because we really are dynamic, cross-functional people. So when we were able to develop these agile teams and agile cultures, I think our workplace is just so much more advanced and authentic."

Building and retaining a strong talent network is increasingly important in a market where organizations need strong employees more than applicants need job openings. In this candidate-focused environment, prioritizing employee engagement and leveraging brand equity ensures companies continue to attract top talent. With AI, it's easier for CHROs to keep tabs on all components of talent networks, including applicants, current employees, and alumni.

The traditional talent network philosophy and tools will no longer work for tomorrow's workforce. It's time to optimize managing and recruiting from robust, modern networks so companies can evolve and thrive in a competitive market.

TOP TALENT TIPS

1. Go back and collate any and all information available on past alumni. Use Eightfold to update their profiles so you have a current repository of your alumni.

2. Identify some of the well-respected people in your company — CEO, founders, senior execs in various functions — and try sending a few nurturing email campaigns to your alumni. Measure the open rates and response rates to determine the efficacy of the outreach message.

3. Review your alumni repository to see how many of them would be a good fit for your current openings.

4. Verify how well these "good fit" candidates did during their past employment at your company. If they did well, you now have proven candidates for open roles.

Chapter 4

The Half-Life of Skills Is Shrinking Fast

"We are limited, but we can push back the borders of our limitations."

Stephen R. Covey

Providing tools to reimagine employee skills and capabilities was a main priority as we developed Eightfold. It's a critical component necessary to solve the talent crisis we find ourselves in — or it could get even worse.

"We are in an interesting time in America, in the sense that on the one hand, we have historically one of the tightest labor markets that we've ever had, and we have a shortage of qualified job seekers to fill all the jobs that we have open in America," said Nisha Biswal, president of the U.S.-India Business Council (USIBC) at the U.S. Chamber of Commerce. "But at the same time that we are in this historically tight labor market with the lowest rates of unemployment and the highest rates of unfilled jobs, there is a lack of sufficient labor to fill those jobs, both at the high end of the spectrum of highly-skilled technical jobs and at the low end of the spectrum of agricultural jobs, or low-skill, low-wage jobs."

When developing the Eightfold platform, we aimed to transform the candidate and enterprise experience, and make it easier to promote internal mobility to try to help mitigate the skill gap that exists externally. It costs at least $5,000 to fill an open position, and nearly a year before the new hire is fully productive, not to mention the company knowledge lost when there's high turnover.

We know that when companies aren't working to retain — *and* retrain — employees, a great deal of money, time, and resources are being wasted on replacing them. AT&T is just one example of an organization trying to change that. Will yours be next?

"When you have workers that already possess much of what you need, it makes a lot more sense to retrain them than to go out and hire new workers—who may be more educated—and then wait a year or more for them to get up to speed with how the company operates," Anthony Carnevale, director and research professor of Georgetown University's Center on Education and the Workforce, told CNBC.[18]

There are multiple ways to encourage employee growth and development within an organization. Setting both employee and supervisor expectations that are meaningful and reachable, and setting aside time for training and development activities can help address the growing skills gap. Ensuring managers know how to develop employees, track progress, and importantly, how to provide constructive feedback and mentorship, strengthens the process.

Having a system in place to reimagine current employee skills will transform the talent life cycle as abilities that might have long been associated with one role can now be redirected to entirely new roles or teams or initiatives — if you can imagine it. Eightfold makes it possible to reimagine all of them for your organization, even as it grows and evolves.

The current cycle of hiring for current or applicable skills is broken and ineffective, and results in a never-ending guessing game on both ends. The employee wonders where their future in the company lies, if their skill set

---

[18] Susan Caminiti. "AT&T's $1 billion gambit: Retraining nearly half of its workforce for jobs of the future". CNBC. March 13, 2018.

measures up, and if upward mobility is even possible. When the answers are hazy, it's an easy decision to leave in search of another position. That leaves recruiters and executives wondering why the employee left, before they dive back into the numbers game of modern recruiting. It's a futile cycle.

Eightfold has worked to interrupt the current cycle with detailed internal talent repositories, and allows for in-depth talent management tools to better track and nurture employees.

It's imperative to align staff, employers, and progressive talent management techniques to improve skill development. Re-education, reimagining of how skills can be applied in new contexts, as well as looking past basic qualifications and hiring for potential will help offset the problems presented by a swiftly declining knowledge base.

We frankly don't even know what we don't know yet. Many of the jobs of the future have yet to be created. So how can we hire for them now?

Experts say our current knowledge base has a half-life of about two years, and the speed of technology is outperforming us as humans because of what it can do quickly and effectively. We've moved so quickly as a culture in America and globally, we don't even know the full implications of what all these various platforms are doing to us yet.

That means successful leaders will learn to rework their approach to finding and nurturing adaptable top talent. The days of stagnant qualifications and slow-changing skill sets are far gone. Utilizing AI provides invaluable insights into the potential a company's talent pool possesses, and where that potential can lead you now and in the future.

LOOK INSIDE FIRST

AT&T attracted waves of praise and awe when it announced its bold plan to retrain more than 100,000 current employees instead of outsourcing an entirely new labor force of skilled software and engineering workers. Internal research showed that only about half of AT&T's 250,000 employees possessed the necessary science, engineering, and tech skills needed to move the company forward. It's an all-too familiar predicament for businesses attempting to keep up with the major technological changes of today's world.

When the perception is that current employees aren't meeting expectations — or might not be able to in the near future— should you look inside or outside first?

Success in today's competitive global economy is reliant on constant innovation and diversity in problem-solving, rather than the actual manufacturing of goods, the one-time foundation of America's economy. This requires more collaboration in the workplace, rather than repetitive production tasks, and means the demand for employees with both hard and soft skills has consistently been changing at a more rapid pace than ever before.

Unfortunately, an ability to adapt to change and to learn or "re-skill" are precisely the skill sets employers are most likely to find lacking in candidates and employees. Traditionally, the intuitive step was to swap out under-skilled workers or managers in favor of new hires who possess the desired characteristics or skill sets needed for a particular role or initiative. But every day, more executives are waking up to the fact that this isn't working, and we bet you're one of them. Nurturing, not replacing, talent provides a greater return to businesses in both retained company knowledge and employee loyalty, and ultimately, in fostering the kind of culture your teams need to thrive.

Organizations are struggling to adapt to this idea of internal hiring in part because supportive recruiting infrastructure is lacking. The majority aren't used to fostering internal employee mobility. Recruiting technology reflects that — which is why we have intentionally crafted the Eightfold algorithms to help ease and more intelligently address the process.

Employees are eager to develop new skills that will help elevate their careers, and human resource executives are tired of embarking on a never-ending hunt for new talent. It's entirely possible for employees to relearn the skills needed to succeed in their company, and it's time to make that talent approach less of a reach.

Additionally, learning how to look beyond hard data and carefully curated resumes to spot a candidate's potential, and what soft skills they will bring to the table, will help bypass the issue of irrelevant skills.

THE POWER OF POTENTIAL

The half-life of skills is shrinking fast, and the abilities of new hires may be rendered obsolete within a year, or even a few months. Learning how to hire for potential can provide a competitive edge in the race for top talent.

Varun Kacholia, Eightfold co-founder, shared a relatable experience of a close friend who had applied to LinkedIn five years in a row. Despite having the necessary expertise and qualifications, his resume was lost among the thousands of other applicants — and he never heard back. After years of being ignored, the company reached out and asked if he would ever be interested in working there. Their applicant tracking system (ATS) never identified he had already applied several times.

What kind of growth and innovation (never mind the wasted time and energy by the talent acquisition team) did LinkedIn miss out on by failing to link up with such an interested and qualified candidate?

Shifting to high-potential teams means finding and connecting with high-potential candidates quickly and effectively. Current systems leave that task up to networking. Eightfold's software is the first to combine analysis of publicly available data, internal data repositories, ATS tools, and spreadsheets. Machine learning combined with artificial intelligence technology drastically improves the search and recommendation process, so the right candidates won't be overlooked and potential can be better measured so that they're matched for the right role at the right time.

Although promoting internal mobility is a way of maximizing potential, you will, of course, still need to look outside of your company for new talent from time to time. Hiring solely based on previous experience has long been the status quo, and it used to work. But today's rapidly changing global economy and digital-first ethos calls for a new type of high-potential candidate — one that possesses curiosity, engagement, insight, and motivation.

"I've experienced the difference in having a team with potential over experience," said Abdullah Snobar, the executive director of DMZ, a leading accelerator for tech startups in Canada, in *Forbes*.[19]

"I've found that shifting to a team with potential not only gave employees the chance to prove themselves but also fuelled motivation, which helped the organization soar to new heights. A candidate's career accomplishments are important and cannot be disregarded, but potential also falls in line with company culture fit. Tech companies present industries with innovation. Therefore, they need to create a team that doesn't become intimidated by change or hitting an unbeaten path."

Executive search advisor Claudio Fernández-Aráoz agrees. He's helped companies hire candidates based on both past experience and an intuitive sense of potential, with very different outcomes. In a *Harvard Business Review* article, he writes of the time he hired

---

[19] Abdullah Snobar. "Hiring In Tech: Potential Over Experience". *Forbes*. June 15, 2018. https://www.forbes.com/sites/forbestechcouncil/2018/06/15/hiring-in-tech-potential-over-experience/

a man with all the right credentials to be the CEO of a family-owned electronics retailer.[20]

Despite earning degrees from top schools, and experience working as a successful manager for a world-renowned company, the man had years of lackluster performance in his new role, and was ultimately asked to leave.

"Despite his impressive background and great fit, he could not adjust to the massive technological, competitive, and regulatory changes occurring in the market at the time," Fernández-Aráoz told HBR.

Compare that with his experience hiring for potential, and the outcome differs drastically. In that instance, Fernández-Aráoz was tasked with finding a project manager for a small brewery in Latin America. He narrowed in on a candidate who had no experience in the industry, and lacked knowledge in key areas of expertise.

Other recruiters would have quickly discarded his resume, but Fernández-Aráoz had a feeling the unlikely candidate would succeed in the role. He took a chance, hired him, and that hunch was proven correct. The new hire was rapidly promoted, and became an integral part of the team that transformed the brewery from a small family-owned business to a large, respected organization with an outstanding management team.

---

[20] Claudio Fernández-Aráoz. "21st-Century Talent Spotting". *Harvard Business Review*. June 2014.

The brewery project manager had the potential — the ability, curiosity, and motivation — to adapt and grow in a changing environment. The CEO did not. Alarmingly, this type of concretely qualified, but low-potential, candidate is the one hired more often than not.

Forty-six percent of all new employee hires fail to adapt within 18 months, according to Leadership IQ, and *Harvard Business Review* reports between 40 and 60 percent of new upper management hires fail within 18 months. We already know organizations are hemorrhaging talent, and hiring applicants who are likely to fail at adapting only exacerbates the problem.

---- ∂ ----

Harvard Business Review reports 40-60% of new upper management hires fail within 18 months

So how can we hire for potential based not only on our instincts — but on data built to help us on both an individual level and at scale? What's been stopping us from taking the leap of faith on candidates that might be our greatest assets?

Measuring potential is not always as easy as measuring past success, which may be one reason why companies are slow to adjust to this new recruiting strategy. There's so much more to a person than a list of achievements on a resume. In fact, we often say resumes should essentially become a thing of the past. Fernández-Aráoz recommends mining a candidate's personal and professional history to get a better grasp of his or her potential.

"Conduct in-depth interviews or career discussions, and do thorough reference checks to uncover stories that demonstrate whether the person has (or lacks) these qualities," he told HBR. "For instance, to assess curiosity, don't just ask, 'Are you curious?' Instead, look for signs that the person believes in self-improvement, truly enjoys learning, and is able to recalibrate after missteps."

MOVING THE NEEDLE

As human HR executives searching for the allusive "purple unicorn," we often look at the wrong metric. For example, given that 90% of software engineers have a computer science background, we assume that anyone who does not have a C.S. background would not or could not get into software engineering.

On the other hand, let's say that there is an academic program called "information management." If 80% of the students from this small program have gone on to become software engineers, machine learning will do a great job at recognizing the pattern and predicting the path for others, while humans will completely miss out on this — or perhaps realize it too late.

How does this happen? Humans tend to looking at software engineers in aggregate to see what is in their profiles. A prediction-based AI engine is doing the opposite. It is looking at an individual and seeing what this person is likely to do next to inform what could be a potential larger pool of candidates. It's acknowledging the potential of others to be similarly successful.

Current recruiting technology is so limited that, more often than not, landing a job is dependent upon who you know rather than actual measurable knowledge and skills. It's hard to even find the right candidate, let alone measure their potential. But what if the massive amount of data in the ATS could be much better utilized and analyzed to create a more robust profile to begin with?

In the recruiting world, there is this concept of "trade secrets." Specialized recruiters know where to look for top talent. But the goal of machine learning is to bring this wisdom to everyone — and that's exactly what Eightfold's AI technology is designed to do.

It's especially critical for hiring high-level executives and managers.

"I think the Eightfold technology will be able to get in and understand what people actually did in their jobs — not just what title they had," said Heidrick & Struggles' Kelly O. Kay.

That's important, because recruiters should be able to show they helped grow the business — and we can't do that by just "closing the req."

———————————— ∞ ————————————

"I think the Eightfold technology will be able to get in and understand what people actually did in their jobs — not just what title they had."
— Heidrick & Struggles' Kelly O. Kay

The career of the famous artist Leonardo da Vinci is the quintessential example of hiring for potential, instead of perhaps what would have been the buzzwords found within a resume in his day. When modern recruiting professionals analyzed his CV — get this — it was found to be lacking in a few areas.[21]

Hundreds of years later, we all know that da Vinci was not only extremely talented in multiple arenas, but is highly regarded as the epitome of the renaissance man and as

---

[21] Elizabeth Garone. "Experts critiqued da Vinci's CV. They weren't impressed." *BBC*. 15 April 2016.

a universal genius. But if he were competing in today's labor pool, would he be hired? Probably not. Therein lies the risk of hiring based solely on past experience or text on a resume, and neglecting to look deeper into a candidate's qualities and potential. Imagine how many da Vincis you've missed out on by failing to utilize this important recruiting strategy.

---- ⚮ ----

We all know that Leonardo da Vinci was not only extremely talented in multiple arenas, but is highly regarded as a genius. But if he were competing in today's labor pool, would he be hired? Probably not.

THE CASE FOR RE-EDUCATION

The ability to unlearn old concepts, and quickly master new ones is a vital aspect of talent potential. It's the difference between the employee who is going to fail within 18 months, and the employee who will creatively contribute to the team in an ongoing capacity and will likely be rapidly promoted.

Higher quality data helps illuminate these candidates, and the Eightfold platform allows you to evaluate both potential and experience of applicants, which ultimately leads to smarter hiring choices. Evaluating the potential of new hires to fit into existing teams also boosts their chances to succeed. A survey of C-suite executives found that the majority of external leaders fail because they don't fit in, or work well, with the people on their teams.[22]

This reflects the growing need for curious, adaptable employees who have the soft skills necessary for collaboration and innovation. You can hire someone from the right school who has all the right experience, but if he or she doesn't fit in with, or adapt to, the company culture, they'll probably fail. We already know more and more candidates are willing to job hop, so why compound the talent problem by setting hires up for failure or dissatisfaction?

Finding adequate leaders and culture fits sometimes means hiring the man or woman who, despite having no concrete experience in the field, brings something different to the table. Diversifying communication and leadership styles also improves innovation and team dynamics. Sometimes, it's a matter of unlearning before we can relearn.

Kinney said retraining can help synthesize diverse personalities and skill sets into one productive, cooperative team.

"I would actually love if we could get a re-education when we started a job," he said. "I remember graduating college at Oklahoma State, which is a completely different part of the country, but I remember you did have a stereotype: if you were a white male who was in

---

[22] Jean Martin. "For Senior Leaders, Fit Matters More Than Skill". *Harvard Business Review*. Jan. 17, 2014.

a fraternity, you were guaranteed a job. And that job was in the industrial sector, or some sort of sales, or banking, and you were paid more than a white woman."

Kinney's re-education concept is just one example of giving employees the opportunity to learn new concepts, and unlearn old ones — this time, in the context of unlearning stereotypes and the missing pieces of higher education. This sort of cultural retraining creates dynamic teams, and ensures new employees can better assimilate.

Leaders should be creating collaborative, open-minded work environments, especially for those who might be experiencing culture shock that's unrelated to the work or team itself because of differences in background — which can be isolating. The push for a re-education also mirrors the increasing need for soft skills, like emotional intelligence, in today's workforce. Hiring tolerant, empathetic, and adaptable people, and re-educating employees on the team environment you hope to foster, are important ways to combat the shrinking half-life of skills.

Technology and tools come and go, but the people carrying out the company's mission are the ones who create sustainable change. Investing in them means investing in the future you wish to see.

Moreover, both young people and older, more experienced employees are pushing for continuous skill development in their careers to stay competitive — and your offerings could be a big draw in attracting top talent. Millennials in particular are attracted by the prospect of ongoing learning opportunities, and employers are using the "ability to learn and progress" to leverage their brand in new ways.

Additionally, collaborating with higher-education institutions to offer training and education programs to employees helps workers gain the foundational and technical skills they need, and employers are increasingly willing to invest in such programs.

An Economist Intelligence Unit report found that 71 percent of the executives surveyed cited increased employee loyalty and higher retention rates as the main incentives for investing in postsecondary education and training programs. The increased employee effectiveness resulting from this investment in training also provided a greater return to the company.[23]

But there's still a gap between what employees are looking for and their perception of how well their companies are listening. The biggest change happening in the youngest part of our workforce? They want to learn quickly and be utilized fully.

Only one third of millennials think their skills are being used well by their employers, according to a Deloitte study. Forty-two percent said they would want to leave a job if they feel they aren't learning fast enough.

Even more eyebrow-raising, the same study found almost all CEOs agree digital technologies are causing

---

[23] The Economist Intelligence Unit. (2014). "Closing the Skills Gap: companies and colleges collaborating for change."

disruptive change in their company, and 70 percent of CEOs said their organization does not possess the skills to adapt.[24] Whether it's a new hire, or someone who has been with the company for years, the half-life of skills is so short that both will inevitably need some level of retraining in the months and years ahead.

LEADERSHIP MATTERS

So how can we provide the tools needed for employees to adapt to an ever-changing, diverse, digital workplace?

More than a third of workers in the U.S. said they have done nothing to upskill in the past year, according to Randstad's 2017 Workmonitor survey. The same study found that 67 percent of employees wanted more training to help maintain relevant skills. Harvard Business Review looked further into this training gap, and discovered that supervisor support played a significant role in career development.[25]

---

[24] Christie Smith and Stephanie Turner, *The Millennial majority is transforming your culture*, Deloitte, 2016, pp. 1–15, https://www2.deloitte.com/content/dam/Deloitte/us/Documents/about-deloitte/us-millennial-majority-will-transform-your-culture.pdf, accessed December 21, 2016

[25] David W. Ballard. "Managers Aren't Doing Enough to Train Employees of the Future". *Harvard Business Review.* November 14, 2017.

More than a third of workers in the U.S. said they have done nothing to upskill in the past year, according to Randstad's 2017 Workmonitor survey.

Employees reported feeling more supported by their supervisor when they were provided with opportunities to develop the technical, management, and leadership skills they believe they will need in the future. Not only does training help company productivity, it also protects against high turnover rates, since we know that employees are more likely to remain at a company if they feel challenged and supported.

However, more men than women reported receiving opportunities to develop the technical, soft, or leadership skills they'll need in the future.[26] The American Psychology Association surveyed 1,076 employees in the U.S., and found that 60 percent of men said their employer provides opportunities to develop management and leadership skills, as opposed to 47 percent of women. Seventy-five percent of men said their company values training and development, while only 61 percent of women said the same.

When unconscious bias gets in the way of equal training opportunities, executives aren't harnessing the full

---

[26] American Psychological Association Survey of 1,076 full-time and part-time employees in the US 2017

potential and power of their talent pool. Clearly, that is not something you can afford to do when the half-life of skills is quickly shrinking.

Knowing the challenges CHROs face in attracting and nurturing talent, we developed the Eightfold platform to more effectively reimagine skills and how to hold onto top performers, while reducing unconscious bias not only when you hire talent, but as that talent grows and evolves within your organization.

That means someone who may have gone unnoticed or without a promotion before would instead be given opportunities early, often, and always to be challenged and engaged.

It's sink or swim at this stage of rapid digital disruption, and the executives who learn how to thrive in this environment will be quick to recruit and retrain employees based on potential.

TOP TALENT TIPS

1. Encourage your employees to learn new capabilities and skills, and when they do, reward them with career progression and share their stories internally. This fosters a culture of learning.

2. Encourage and perhaps help develop a virtual skillshare or mentorship program where employees at all levels can provide specific expertise to colleagues across physical locations and functional teams.

3. Publicly acknowledge and reward employees who are acquiring new skills. This will set the tone of what the executives care about in your organization.

4. Do a 9-box exercise of your team with an eye on what you need to get done over the next 12 months. And see which of the team members you would still keep, who needs some help in contributing effectively to team or company objectives and who is not really in a position to help.

Chapter 5

Rethinking the Candidate Experience

---- ∞ ----

"I'd said to my partner Stedman,

'What am I going to talk about

for ten days and ten nights at Nelson

Mandela's house?' Stedman said,

'Why don't you try listening?'"

Oprah Winfrey

At the beginning of this book, we outlined some of the issues that have led to the current talent management crisis in which we've found ourselves. Job hopping. The gig economy. Diversity struggles. These are just a few of the complex problems we're facing as executives.

But the level of pain and frustration is perhaps nowhere more apparent than for the candidates themselves — and that pain is trickling upward to the C-suite quickly as top employees move from one job to the next and hiring managers struggle to keep up, stunting growth and wreaking havoc on the company's bottom line.

We know that fixing such a complex problem requires both executive commitment and sophisticated technology, not to mention a greater understanding of significant amounts of data at our disposal.

CANDIDATES WANT CHANGE

In our study conducted with Harris Interactive Research in 2018, Eightfold found that 56% of job candidates have changed employers in the last 3 years and 84% are looking for a new position either with another company or with their current employer.

Let that sink in for a moment. More than half of the candidates we surveyed have looked for a new job in the past three years, and furthermore, our data shows that for those who qualify as 'top talent,' the numbers are even worse: nearly half of **top** talent (47%) leave within 2 years of joining an organization and 61% move on after 3 years.

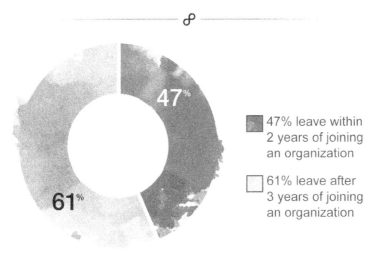

47%

61%

47% leave within
2 years of joining
an organization

61% leave after
3 years of joining
an organization

Source: Talent Intelligence & Management Report 2018, Harris Media Survey

Retention Rate from Date of Hire for Top Talent

So what are some of the biggest reasons employees cite for leaving a job, according to our research? Compensation is a factor, but candidates also cite other important drivers such as feeling that their work is not valued and issues with management. Less than half (48%) rate their organization as effective in specific areas related to talent management such as career planning, internal mobility, and mentoring programs.

That means compensation is just one of the factors that compels people to look outside. Since most companies have fallen into the habit of paying more for talent that has been developed by others, we are not serving our current employees. We need to provide career and growth opportunities in a proactive fashion, so that employees feel appreciated and rewarded for their contributions long before they consider leaving — and can feel confident that their current employer provides the most fruitful career path now and in the future.

More than half of candidates believe that there is an overall lack of diversity in their current organization, particularly in terms of qualified, diverse talent.

They also report that more work needs to be done for employers to become more effective in both talent acquisition and talent retention in general: 70% agree that finding talent is a key challenge in their organization.

The good news? We believe we can solve this crisis by focusing on the candidate and his or her needs before, during, and after joining an organization.

PEOPLE WORK FOR PEOPLE

As diversity and inclusion efforts continue to be an important part of HR initiatives nationwide, AI can be a powerful tool that can help provide 'masked' screening. The technology, when used correctly, will reveal which applicants have the most relevant expertise and are likely to be an advantageous fit for available positions within the company by correlating skills to mathematical algorithms without a photo or name attached to them, removing potential for human bias.

Just how important is diversity in the future of talent management? It's at the top of the list, and for good reason. In our recent study conducted by Harris Interactive, we surveyed both candidates and C-suite executives. We've highlighted some of the responses from candidates in the sections above, but here's what executives had to say.

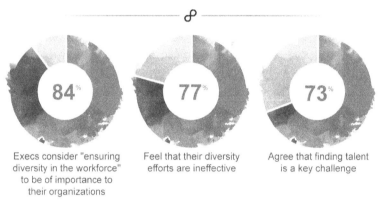

| Execs consider "ensuring diversity in the workforce" to be of importance to their organizations | Feel that their diversity efforts are ineffective | Agree that finding talent is a key challenge |

Source: Talent Intelligence & Management Report 2019, Harris Media Survey

Talent retention is of utmost importance to C-Level execs

- 84% of execs consider "ensuring diversity in the workforce" to be of importance to their organizations
- 77% feel that their diversity efforts are ineffective
- **Talent retention** is of utmost importance to C-level execs
- 73% agree that finding talent is a key challenge

AI is an essential tool in retaining and promoting a diverse workforce. While these technologies focus on identifying a strong match between a role and candidates based on public and company-specific data, AI also helps create more efficient and fair opportunities for promotions. We are constantly working on collecting more data to make our AI smarter and to present results in the best, most understandable and actionable format.

Some of our current clients, such as AdRoll and DigitalOcean, are using our proprietary AI process (which complies with all EEOC regulations) to create more diverse organizations with significant results. Studies have shown that effective diversity initiatives tend to improve business outcomes — including everything from more creativity to better relationships with customers.[27]

We'll dive more into the topic of reducing and eliminating human bias with AI in our chapter on **"Bias"** later on.

We're also working on further integrating AI into the HR performance evaluation process so that we can help make recommendations on the potential for long-term success in a particular role or company. It's critical that AI works for you, not the other way around.

But these insights don't mean anything without the human touch and proper analysis to drive smart decisions. The notion that "people work for people" is particularly important when it comes to recruiting and retaining diverse candidates — and helping to ensure they feel empowered and recognized each step of the way.

"Millennials are loyal to people, not necessarily companies," said Ciara Ennis, a marketing manager in

---

[27] https://www.ciphr.com/advice/5-reasons-diverse-workforce-matters/

the U.K. "I know if I'm working for people that value my work, that I'll always have somewhere to go."

By utilizing AI effectively in HR recruitment, diversity initiatives, and in employee retention, businesses can drive innovation. The insights gained from creating robust profiles of potential candidates, employees, and companies means that companies can make highly beneficial conclusions when it comes to hiring, performance evaluations and promotions more quickly and with less financial strain.

DON'T SETTLE FOR MEDIOCRITY

One of my cofounder Varun's favorite phrases is, "don't settle for mediocrity."

In talent recruitment and management, what does that look and feel like? To me, it means looking for people who are hungry. People who are agile. People who are forward-thinking. People who want to learn. (More on this in **Chapter 4: The Half-Life of Skills Is Shrinking Fast.**)

But we must have the best and widest possible pool of talent in order to find those would-be unicorns and help them realize you're invested in helping them stay at the top of their game. That means refocusing and doubling down on diversity and inclusion efforts, says Atlassian's Aubrey Blanche.

"There's a mathematical fact that where you lack diversity, you have tolerated mediocrity in your hiring process," she said. "People often talk about the trade off between diversity and lowering the bar, but mathematically speaking, because brilliance and talent are not distributed just among particular groups, diversity — or what I call building balanced teams — is actually the outcome of having really high hiring standards."

ôP

"Because brilliance and talent are not distributed just among particular groups, diversity — or what I call building balanced teams — is actually the outcome of having really high hiring standards."
— Aubrey Blanche, Global Head of Diversity & Belonging at Atlassian

I always say that if you think you're building a $10 million company, that's what you'll build.

If, on the other hand, you think there's potential for much, much more — imagine where you and your business could go?

The possibilities of human potential and the importance of our collective desire to find meaningful work is at the heart of what we do. But for too long, a number of companies have taken human capital for granted and now we must face the music and create a better way forward for the current and the next generation.

The current mindset for too many organizations is what I call the "leech" method: extract what an employee knows, suck the life out of them, and four years later, do the same with a new crop of people. It's exploiting people versus helping them grow.

We believe — and our data proves – that you simply won't survive with that approach any longer.

Take Google as an example. Around six or seven years ago, Google was sucking all of the talent out while Facebook was trying to attract new talent to help them invest in mobile, so they decided to build talent in-house rather than look outside. That's how these companies are doing it today; they've learned that to continue to innovate, people cannot be taken for granted. They cannot be permitted to be placed in mediocre positions. And we all must do better to create opportunities for greatness from the time of application to the time of exit.

It's always easy to blame someone else, and we tend to not realize that talent management is not right until it's too late.

So what can we do better? Take the ownership to create change now.

A MORE MODERN APPROACH

Don Robertson, CHRO at Northwestern Mutual and an expert in global human resources, is advocating for a modern approach to the candidate experience from the moment someone applies to a new role with your company. Most important, he says, is that it aligns with your company's ethos as a whole.

"If you create the experience, whether it's the onboarding or the interview process itself, or the whole process of recruiting — if it doesn't feel modern and it doesn't feel like it's 2019 and beyond, you're not going to attract the right kind of people," he said.

For example, Robertson said using a paper application or taking too long to respond at all can be major red flags to a potential candidate that your organization is not with the times — and the little things could have a negative impact on recruitment efforts just as much as other steps you're taking to build the relationship.

He also explained that the millennial generation — which we'll dive into more deeply in the section **"Thriving With Millennials"** later on — is interested in making an impact now, not later.

When he launched a women's program at his prior company, for example, he tapped junior-level staff members to lead the effort rather than senior-level executives.

"I went to two women that were potentially going to be, I thought, future leaders and put them in a leadership position early on so they could start to develop some of those skills," he said. "We got them exposure to senior leadership so that they would start to get to know who they were, and now all of a sudden everybody wanted to be on the women's network — even guys."

JOB DESCRIPTIONS ARE BROKEN

Career websites that have poorly written job descriptions (which is most of them), and that don't make it easy for people interested in working for them to find the right role easily are putting their companies at a competitive disadvantage in an already tight labor market. They may not have created the talent crisis, but they are definitely not solving it either.

All current systems have been designed to solve for the enterprise, as if we are managing widgets moving through a supply chain, rather than people with hearts and minds. Widgets don't have career aspirations. Widgets don't ask for work-life balance and acknowledgment and appreciation for their efforts.

Our employees do. The candidates we want to attract do. We forget that this is a candidate's market today — and if you're someone who has the talent that others are looking for, you can dictate the terms of your employment. If you are learning new and relevant skills — you can pick who you want to work for, where, and when.

Here at Eightfold, one of the most significant ways we're working on creating change in talent acquisition and management is with the industry's first-ever recommendation engine designed to match job descriptions with a job seeker's experience AND capabilities to make a meaningful career path possible at every level.

Introduced in 2018, the first Talent Intelligence Platform harnesses the power of AI and search, creating a rich, personalized candidate-facing experience, rooted in a deep understanding of the candidate's background.

We estimate that nearly 80 percent of today's job seekers apply to the wrong job because companies lack the ability to tailor the details of job descriptions to best present the true roles and responsibilities of a particular position. I like to call this the "free lunch" phenomenon. Why are we touting "free lunch" in our job descriptions when that can't be the core function of a job, nor is it one of the key draws in attracting or retaining qualified talent?

This kind of ineffective communication before a candidate has even joined the organization ultimately results in high turnover and those frequent job changes reported in our survey, which continue to be one of the biggest contributors to today's talent crisis.

What's worse: as a result of ineffective job descriptions, we estimate that less than five percent of applicants who do end up applying for open positions are worth pursuing because they've been mismatched.

All of this adds up to a surplus of available opportunities within any given organization, wasted time and resources on the wrong people, plus a lack of innovation and growth for individuals and companies, all while the majority of candidates complain about finding the right role.

We aim to fix a key flaw in the current system: match open positions to specific candidate capabilities. But importantly, we've taken it a step further. We match the candidate's capabilities to the *next* job in their career.

─────────── ∂ ───────────

We match the candidate's capabilities
to the next job in their career

We're invested in helping candidates reimagine their futures — using predictive technology and robust data sets to help them discover their full potential with sophisticated insights into career paths that will be most meaningful for individuals and organizations.

This is groundbreaking and represents a whole new model of thinking about hiring.

With this data, companies can find, engage, and motivate their best people to help them achieve business and personal success. We're focused three core capabilities: talent, personalization, and artificial intelligence.

- **Talent.** We're creating a comprehensive talent network unique to an organization by aggregating all internal and external data for an enterprise – from applicants to alumni – which is currently siloed across many different domains and solutions. This network is usually 200 to 250 times the number of active employees in a company at any given time. For example, if your company has 10,000 employees, your talent pool should be 2 million to 2.5 million candidates. With AI, you can evaluate every single person in this talent pool for every single open job position. In a fraction of a second. This is simply not possible with humans.
- **Personalization.** By providing intelligence on people's capabilities and future potential, organizations can personalize recruitment efforts both internally and externally. This empowers hiring teams and managers to be more effective in matching talent to the right opportunities at the right time, ultimately improving candidate relevance and engaging at-risk employees to avoid attrition.
- **Machine Learning.** Powered by purpose-built deep learning models, the Eightfold platform continuously learns from all data, engagement and decisions in the enterprise to predict future roles and career

alternatives, and supports diversity and inclusion initiatives.

Here's how it works: our proprietary deep learning considers relevant work experience, educational background, skills, roles, and multitudes of additional attributes to match a candidate to the right opportunity within an organization. After a candidate uploads a resume or links to an online resume page, the Eightfold platform creates an enriched profile with additional, publicly available data, to match the candidate with open positions at a company.

Within seconds, the recommendation engine suggest jobs that best fit the candidate — and takes erroneous guesswork out of the picture. The technology is available for employees who want to refer someone to an organization as well as new candidates applying to a company.

A BETTER MATCH

As we've explained, AI can help bridge the talent gap by providing candidates and employers with forward-looking insights that reveal not only what someone has done, but powerful data on what their full potential could be. With this data, companies can find, engage, and motivate their best people to help them achieve personal and business success.

One of the most important and exciting ways we're working on harnessing the power of AI in the HR field is in the recruitment of talented candidates. There's a desire — perhaps more than ever — to find meaningful work that fulfills and energizes us, and to find employers and colleagues who share our values and help us be our best selves.

These may sound like lofty goals, but they're achievable today. AI and machine-learning technology is progressing at incredible speeds, and our ability to process and analyze information more effectively is one of the keys to helping to solve the talent gap in recruiting, especially when it comes to helping people find a job that's a much better match.

Using AI, we can predict the potential of a particular candidate and his or her ability to learn a new skill required on the job — seeing far beyond what he or she has done in the past.

That's where the magic happens. We can actually put exemplary candidates in the roles that align best with business needs.

This highly effective process is particularly critical for companies hiring talent at scale, because it helps HR professionals systematically and proactively identify the best candidates, greatly increasing the number of candidates that might be considered by using sophisticated, personalized algorithms to fit a business' specific needs. That means a much more diverse pool of talented potential employees will be organized and vetted for openings now and in the future, saving time, money, and resources.

THE NEW CANDIDATE PROFILE

Nearly any challenge facing HR professionals today can be solved by having access to better data and improved insights into finding and retaining the most talented candidates and helping them to find the most meaningful work possible. Used responsibly, AI technology has the ability to greatly reduce human bias in the recruitment and retention process, and most importantly, to create a happier, more diverse workforce — the backbone of a productive and progressive society.

By utilizing AI effectively in HR recruitment, diversity initiatives, and in employee retention, businesses can drive innovation. The insights gained from creating robust profiles of potential candidates, employees, and companies means that companies can make highly beneficial conclusions when it comes to hiring, performance evaluations and promotions more quickly and with less financial strain.

So given all of the data now at our disposal, how do we build a better profile of the type of individual we'd like to have on our team?

"One of the advantages the Eightfold product is it can look at the present moment and historically look at all candidates who have applied for positions in your organization, as well as reach out into the larger market, and pull profiles on potential candidates that match your skill and competency or engagement criteria that you're using that says, 'this is the ideal profile for this particular role or job or position,'" said Russell Williams, President & Founder, HR Global Link.

"You're now able to do that in real time with an application that's mobile — where you can now see who's available and understand who's come into the organization that you may have overlooked or you may want to go back and look at, as well as other potential candidates, all of which can be customized and driven by the software application."

The bottom line? AI can help companies, recruiters, and hiring managers look beyond what they have seen and expose them to a larger set of talent. Humans are good at analyzing, but not at processing large amounts of data. As a result, we keep narrowing down our criteria and remember only the most *popular* things.

For example, every recruiter and hiring manager knows about MIT. Very few know about Wellesley (an all-female college) or Olin college, which are both excellent schools.

These are some of the top colleges in the country, but because of their small size, they're not as well-known and therefore often overlooked. Further, bias is already ingrained in using names of schools as key criteria, Atlassian's Aubrey Blanche says.

"Data tells us that the number one factor that predicts whether or not you go to a top 25 university in the United States is how much money your parents make," she noted.

If you're ignoring a great all-female college — or better yet, someone who attended a school off your radar completely — you are bound to have a diversity challenge before hiring even begins, perhaps without knowing or realizing it.

⁓ ∞ ⁓

TOP TALENT TIPS

1. Consider implementing a blind screening process and/or tool for talent acquisition

2. Create meaningful benchmarks for measuring the progress and success of diversity and inclusion efforts — retention/promotion of diverse candidates, engagement, etc.

3. Organize a regular focus group or time for employees to come together to talk openly about cultural issues that might be affecting performance or productivity — create a task force to help resolve these issues in a fair and sensitive manner

4. Ensure employees and managers have access to a robust internal application system informed by AI that creates sophisticated matching opportunities early and often for top talent to move to new roles easily and confidently.

⁓ ∞ ⁓

Chapter 6

Bias Is a Four-Letter Word

"I'm not the woman president of Harvard. I'm the president of Harvard."

Drew Gilpin Faust

Most of us mean well, but *all* of us are biased. It's part of being human. People have biases for gender, race, age, schools, religion, disabilities, sexual orientation.

As we've developed the deep learning algorithms at Eightfold to solve a number of talent acquisition and talent management challenges, reducing human bias has been top of mind. Diversity and inclusion initiatives have gone from "nice-to-haves" to must-have imperatives, and we're committed to designing thoughtful solutions that can help organizations create real change and a positive experience for their most talented employees.

Of course, there are countless studies and data to back up the financial and cultural benefits of having a more diverse workforce — some of which we'll outline here. Plus, not only has the word become a popular buzzword in job descriptions or company mission statements, but fair and equitable treatment of job applications is required by federal and state law in the United States, especially in terms of protected classes, such as race, gender, disability, age, and sexual orientation.

But none of this matters if the leaders at the top of your organization aren't on board with the moral imperative associated with embracing true diversity and inclusion from top to bottom. And, most importantly, we all must know how we'll make change happen, how we'll measure its success, and how to make adjustments as we grow and evolve.

BIAS IS A FOUR-LETTER WORD

As we alluded to earlier, diversity is no longer just a convenient buzzword or an item on a checklist. Bias, just like some other choice four-letter words not permitted in a polite work conversation, is simply unacceptable. But of course, being the accomplished CHRO or CEO that you are, you already know this. So how can we move forward?

People have now realized the value in a diverse, multicultural and dynamic workplace. As well as just being the right thing to do, diverse executive boards generate better financial returns[28], and gender-diverse teams are more creative, more productive, and more confident.[29]

For example, McKinsey & Co, a top consulting agency, studied over 1,000 companies across 12 countries and found that firms in the top quartile for gender diversity were a fifth more likely to have above-average profits than those in the bottom quartile.

Although women make up more than half of the U.S. population, and 57 percent of college graduates are female, fewer women tend to be hired even into entry-level positions. At each step of the talent pipeline, women are more and more underrepresented.[30]

---

[28] https://www.mckinsey.com/business-functions/organization/our-insights/is-there-a-payoff-from-top-team-diversity

[29] https://www.ncwit.org/sites/default/files/resources/impactgenderdiversitytechbusinessperformance_print.pdf

[30] https://www.marketwatch.com/story/in-corporate-america-a-shockingly-low-number-of-women-make-it-to-the-c-suite-2018-04-30

In the C-suite, only 20 percent of the talent is female.

For women of color, that statistic is much worse. Despite making up 19 percent of the total U.S. population, only 3 percent of women of color are represented at the executive level.[31]

In 2015, women held 57 percent of jobs, but in computing, held only a quarter of jobs, according to the National Center for Women & Information Technology. And while this number is low, it's even lower for women of color. Black women held only 3 percent of these jobs, while Latinas held only 1 percent.[32]

These statistics are discouraging and incredibly frustrating for women as they progress in their careers, and rightly so.

Elle, 27, a Silicon Valley–based marketing director, finds the lack of gender diversity disheartening.

"I think when I look at who occupies the leadership positions at the companies where I've worked or my friends have worked, it is overwhelmingly male." she said. "And sadly, I know that is not unique to Silicon Valley, or the rest of the world. So it feels like being in the C-suite is almost unattainable if you're a woman."

Because the data shows that all too often women don't have the same opportunities as men right from the

---

[31] https://womenintheworkplace.com/ p.4
[32] https://www.ncwit.org/sites/default/files/resources/womenintech_facts_fullreport_05132016.pdf

beginning of their careers, progression can be difficult at best, and unattainable at worst. Clearly, more work is needed at the talent acquisition stage continuing on through to promotion, engagement, re-engagement after temporary leave (such as maternity), and with alumni. We'll address each of these important areas in this section.

CULTURE MATTERS

Experts in the field of diversity and inclusion (D&I) have explained to me the difference between Diversity, Inclusion and Belonging, and I think it bears repeating here:

- **Diversity** means you are invited to a party.
- **Inclusion** means you are invited to dance on the dance floor at the party.
- **Belonging** means you feel comfortable dancing however you want to and you're not worried about what others will think of your dancing.

Belonging is the pinnacle of all of our dedicated efforts to create real change when it comes to D&I initiatives. It's something we're incredibly passionate about at Eightfold because AI is the technology that could bring us closer together.

"I think part of what makes this really exciting is because it means we can actually accelerate progress," said Global Head of Diversity & Belonging at Atlassian, Aubrey Blanche. "Something like Eightfold can actually help people set up a system that aligns with their intention of what they believe about people and who they want to hire, that can literally interrupt the biases they have been predisposed to. Because you can't necessarily rewire someone's brain. There are subtle ways you can change those biases, but that's with a long term and high effort process."

— ♂ —

"*Eightfold can help people set up a system that aligns with their intention of what they believe about people and who they want to hire, that can literally interrupt the biases they have been predisposed to — because you can't necessarily rewire someone's brain.*"
— Aubrey Blanche, Global Head of Diversity & Belonging at Atlassian

For Sona Venkat, who currently serves as Senior Vice President and General Manager of Strategy and Business Development at Microsoft, and has worked in senior roles at SAP and Oracle, she's credited much of her success to mentorship as she's climbed the ranks in largely male-driven organizations.

Even though she was living and working remotely from big business hubs like Silicon Valley and New York, she was given growing responsibilities that allowed her to show leadership potential early on.

"It start[ed] with one person who took the time and effort to invest in me as somebody who was capable, who was reliable, but also who was motivated," she said.

However, she adds it wasn't always easy.

"I come from a generation of women that there weren't enough female mentors," Venkat said. "I feel it is my responsibility [to mentor the next generation of women]."

In fact, she feels it's an imperative all C-suite level executives must make a priority as diversity and inclusion numbers continue to reflect either dismal movement or only incremental change for a number of top companies.

"It's not just a problem, it is a crisis that is at the C-level agenda," Sona said. "We're embarrassed. We're compared to our peers, but even our peers are not doing well. It's embarrassing, and it is a crisis."

Being an ethnically-diverse organization is beneficial to the bottom line, as proven by countless studies. Hiring people from diverse backgrounds (education, ethnicity, age, gender, (dis)ability) is — in theory — one of the easiest ways to improve profitability and problem-solving.

As Elle, one of our millennial experts puts it, "If everyone is from the same place, everyone is going to have similar ideas."

AGE IS JUST A NUMBER

A diversity problem that is often overlooked is ageism. Human bias, perception, and our propensity for generalization come into play most frequently here. Just like Goldilocks in the "Three Little Pigs" fairytale, we're often looking for someone who falls within our set expectations — for what we believe will be "just right" in terms of fit for a particular role based on our own background and experience. Goldilocks was in search of the perfect bed and bowl of porridge —and we're all in the search for the perfect job candidate.

But whether we perceive a job candidate or internal employee to be "too young" and therefore too inexperienced for a role, or "too old" and seen as not innovative, many talented, hard-working people are often discriminated against for their age and not given opportunities to contribute.

How often do you think your company has missed out on talent because of age perceptions? What kind of growth or innovation might your competitor have achieved as a result?

For young people in particular, they often find that their opinions are overlooked in the workplace, or feel that they're not taken as seriously as their older peers, despite their education or level of dedication to their work.

"I had just come out of university, and it was perceived that my opinions probably weren't as valid," said Ciara

Ennis, 28, a marketing manager in the U.K., and one of our millennial experts. "This was a year's contract position and it took about six months for me to really prove myself, to show the team the value I brought an that was a valuable part of the team."

Despite being qualified, Ennis felt she was not taken seriously for six months. For this generation of talent, that's just too long. And for this era of digital transformation and ultra-fast pace of skills that must be learned or relearned faster than ever, it's way too long. In Ennis's case, the company essentially missed out on valuable input for half of her contract, effectively throwing money down the drain. What executive would actually do that on purpose?

That's where AI comes in especially handy, Blanche said: "What really great AI does in this space, is it helps us overcome that human limitation to help us do what we were trying to do in the first place."

Still, Elle, one of our other millennial experts, also finds her youth a hindrance, especially when looking for new roles.

"I have gone from being an intern to being a director in five years," she said. "Trying to find a director position outside of the company is proving more difficult because people look at my resume and think 'she's too young to be a director,' and will offer different levels of that job without even meeting me first."

MASKED SCREENING CAN BE A GAME-CHANGER

One of the most important ways Elle's frustrations could be solved would be through the use of AI to provide masked screening. When used correctly, it reveals the best candidate for the job based on relevant experience and potential, regardless of their race, gender, age, sexual orientation or disabilities. By correlating skills to mathematical algorithms, there is no possibility of human bias, all while complying with EEOC regulations.

For Daniel Doody, head of EMEA recruitment at Zendesk, who previously worked at AdRoll, said the use of masked screening has been a game-changer.

AdRoll reported improved search results and ultimately improved diversity and inclusion outcomes with the use of Eightfold's platform to both find and nurture potential talent.

"Understanding that we are human and this process is naturally fraught with errors, AI enhances our lives," Doody said. "From a recruiter's standpoint, that means freeing up time and making us more efficient."

ACKNOWLEDGING DIFFERENCES

Some of those errors begin in our own circle of friends. Our social networks tend to act as extensions of ourselves, going so far as to mirror our gender, race, political beliefs, and alma maters. If we keep searching in our social networks for potential hires, we will likely keep hiring more of the same.

It's a common trend for employers to hire from their alumni networks when searching for new talent. While not always a bad idea, if we continually hire people who went to the same college we risk hiring more of the same.

Never branching outside of a certain group will slow our march towards building a more diverse team, as people with similar experiences and backgrounds will continue working together.

With AI, we can employ similar requirements to filter candidates, including background, school, experience, and capabilities. However, the software can also look for diversity within candidates who fit that ideal profile. Now you are hiring people with similar capabilities, but from much more diverse backgrounds. This accelerates the journey toward a more diverse and productive organization.

And culturally, this opens our mind to other people, who may not have the same background as ours, but are equally capable of achieving great outcomes. We learn not to judge the book by its cover, and we learn how to scale an organization without being limited by our own backgrounds. AI allows you to cast a wide net, and also to look for fairly precise requirements in a candidate, and succeed in finding them.

INCLUSION

So now that you've recruited diverse talent, how will you help them thrive? Internal mobility, and meaningful, inclusive culture.

Not only can AI make hiring diverse workforces easier, but it can help track progress of those important inclusivity initiatives, including tracking retention and promotion.

It is not just about hiring, but companies should also focus on how to provide their workforces with internal mobility to make their work lives fulfilling. CEOs and CHROs can build diverse, open and inclusive organizations by using the power of AI to transparently implement diversity at every level across the company for better business outcomes.

TOP TALENT TIPS

1. Consider implementing a masked screening process and/or tool for talent acquisition.

2. Create meaningful benchmarks for measuring the progress and success of diversity and inclusion efforts — retention/promotion of diverse candidates, engagement, etc.

3. Organize a regular focus group or time for employees to come together to talk openly about cultural issues that might be affecting performance or productivity — create a task force to help resolve these issues in a fair and sensitive manner.

4. Ensure employees and managers have access to a robust internal application system informed by AI that creates sophisticated matching opportunities early and often for top talent to move to new roles easily and confidently.

Chapter 7
Thriving With Millennials

❧

"As coaches, our job is to nudge them in the right direction, guide them, but we don't control them. They determine their own fate."

Steve Kerr

WHO ARE MILLENNIALS?

As we work on solving the talent crisis with the help of AI, we'd be remiss if we didn't acknowledge some of the major shifts in demographics that are impacting how we hire and manage people.

Since entering the workforce during the past decade, the millennial generation — which the Pew Research Center broadly defines as those who were born between 1980 and 1996 — has had arguably the most profound impact on the way we do business and how we think about the work we do in America. They currently comprise the largest sector of the workforce at about 35%, according to Pew, and that number is expected to get closer to 50% by 2020, according to researchers.[33]

But just who exactly are millennials, and how do they think? What motivates them and drives them to succeed? Most importantly, how can we best engage millennials from the moment they've applied for an open position with our firms, and best help support their growth?

First, let's take a look at what shapes some of their thinking. According to Michael Dimock at the Pew Research Center, millennials were old enough to understand the significance of the 9/11 terror attacks when they happened, grew up during the political climate of the Iraq and Afghanistan wars, came of age when the youth vote drove the election of the first American black president, came of age and entered the workforce

---

[33] Pew Research Center. http://www.pewresearch.org/fact-tank/2019/01/17/where-millennials-end-and-generation-z-begins/

during the 2008 Great Recession, and had their lives shaped by technology as the internet exploded in the early 2000s.

Millennials, the most diverse generation yet, have had their lives shaped by technology as the internet exploded in the early 2000s

They're also the most diverse generation to join the workforce yet: more than 40% of them are nonwhite, and many of them were among those voters who helped elect the nation's first black president in Barack Obama in 2008. But the recession and student loan debt have also colored their purview, causing many millennials to delay marriage and buying a home, among other more traditional milestones that generations before them embraced.

HOW DO MILLENNIALS THINK ABOUT WORK?

Given their diverse backgrounds, many millennials are eschewing tradition in more ways than one. Not only are they saying no to marriage and yes to singledom at higher rates than ever before, they're also embracing more open and flexible lifestyles in general — and that, of course, includes work.

Millennials tend to be highly educated, but with a collective $1 trillion in student loan debt, we might think they're eager to find not only meaningful work but financial stability after graduating from college or graduate school.

But USC demographer Dowell Myers pointed out that while they tend to remain economically cautious, millennials tend to also remain idealistic and optimistic.

"People ask, aren't young people always optimistic?" said Neil Howe, president of LifeCourse Associates, a consulting firm on generational trends in Great Falls, Va., who, along with a co-author, coined the term 'Millennial.' "The answer is no. Back in the late '70s, young Boomers were the most pessimistic of generations."

So how does that optimism affect the way millennials live and work? For some, there's a stigma associated with what millennials view as a sort of entitlement and the blind naivete that comes along with it, while for others, it's what will help save us all from intolerance. Some managers struggle to find common ground, while others attempt to appease their unique needs as a means of ensuring loyalty.

This divergence in approach can make the job of hiring and managing millennials a challenge — but not impossible.

"Millennials have a can-do attitude about tasks at work and look for feedback about how they are doing frequently—even daily and certainly weekly," noted Susan Heathfield, a management consultant, in a post for The Balance Careers. "Millennials want a variety of tasks and expect that they will accomplish every one of them. Positive and confident, millennials are ready to take on the world."

Most importantly, millennials crave flexibility. Actually, they demand it. According to Bentley University's 2017 "Multi-generational Impacts on the Workplace" report, they tend to be more protective of their time away from work, and value paid parental and family leave more than generations before them.

Deloitte's most recent millennial survey, which is based on the views of more than 10,000 millennials worldwide, indicates that flexibility at work and management's commitment to diversity and inclusion efforts are the two biggest factors in job happiness today.

DIVERSITY MATTERS

We know that diversity and inclusion efforts are top of mind for both C-suite executives and millennial employees alike. But how can we make good on our promise to be more inclusive and to promote diverse talent when we don't have the tools and comprehensive data we need to do so as our organizations grow and evolve?

According to some of our millennial experts, we needn't look further than the C-suite itself to get started.

Pointing to General Motors, which was highlighted in the press recently for hiring its first female CFO, Elle said, "I feel like some people read that news and think, 'see! we're getting it right, it's 2018, times have changed. Women are getting the opportunities now.' But the reality is we have such a long way to go. Of the Fortune 500 companies, only 25 of them have women CEOs. It's just not good enough."[34]

Clearly, more work needs to be done, and millennial job candidates and employees are the ones who will push us to find ways we can all work together to build more diverse teams from the top down.

Remember: diversity means diversity.

While many of us think of gender or race when we think about creating more inclusive work cultures, it's important to consider our hiring practices when it comes to people

---

[34] https://www.businessinsider.com/fortune-500-companies-women-ceos-2018-8

of all ages, abilities and disabilities, and religious or family backgrounds.

But what about educational backgrounds? How can we be sure we're not leaving qualified candidates on the sidelines because they attended a smaller school or perhaps one we just haven't heard of yet?

FINDING MEANINGFUL WORK

Despite some of the negative stereotypes that surround the young people of today, there are a number of reasons we must stay tuned in to their unique set of values as they grow into professionals and leaders of the future.

"These are people that want to make an impact, and are going to hold you accountable for what you say," said Don Robertson, Chief Human Resources Officer at Northwestern Mutual. "Your culture needs to match what you say your vision is, and how you want to operate."

For example, one of the most important ways millennials differ from the generation before them is in their passion for finding work that truly fulfills them.

At Eightfold, we couldn't be more excited to help millennials — and employees, managers, and executives of all ages — to do exactly that.

In fact, the name of our company, "Eightfold," is derived from a Buddhist philosophy in which all of your actions and thoughts pursued in a mindful, righteous way can bring about meaningfulness in life.

—— ∂ ——

The name of our company, "Eightfold," is derived from a Buddhist philosophy in which all of your actions and thoughts pursued in a mindful, righteous way can bring meaning to our lives.

Today, Eightfold is viewed and lauded as a "mission-driven" company. But all we are doing is putting our collective expertise to work in solving employment for everyone. The old adage of, "if you like what you do, you will never work a day in your life," applies to all of us at Eightfold — and most acutely, to all millennials. Even for those of us who were not born between 1980 and 1996, we're still embracing this message.

In an article for Psychology Today, Dr. Shawn Meghan Burn pointed to how psychologist Ellen Kossek and her colleagues describe a sustainable workforce[35] as "one whose employees have the positive energy, capabilities, vitality, and resources to meet current and future organizational performance demands while sustaining their economic and mental health on and off the job."

If we're all promoting positive energy in our millennial employees, just imagine the possibilities.

---

[35] "The Sustainable Workforce: Organizational Strategies for Promoting Work-Life Balance and Well-Being." November 2013 (In book: Wellbeing in the Workplace: From Stress to Happiness, Publisher: Wiley-Blackwell, Editors: Cary Cooper, Peter Chen, pp.295-317) via Psychology Today

TOP TALENT TIPS

1. Organize a meet-and-greet event with some of your top millennial talent. Get to know them and their unique interests. Empower and embolden them to take on more leadership tasks or responsibilities.

2. Start a mentorship program with the help of Eightfold's AI talent experience platform.

3. Check in with your brand management and innovation team. According to our millennial experts, they tend to feel more energized when they're working on something cutting-edge.

Chapter 8

What's Next For You?

· ∞ ·

"Change will not come if we wait for some other person or some other time. We are the ones we've been waiting for. We are the change that we seek."

Barack Obama

It's clear that we've reached a crisis in hiring and retaining top talent. There's a shortage of qualified candidates. Labor-intensive processes often means hiring takes too long. An alarming number of jobs are unfilled.

The average person will spend at least 40 years of their life working — and this number will likely go up as the cost of living and the average lifespan increase. With the current trend of job hopping, the average stay at any given job is two to three years. That means we will have about 15 different jobs in our lifetime. Shouldn't we make every one of these opportunities count? We have 15 chances to achieve our career, monetary, and personal growth aspirations.

We believe in maximizing every single one.

THE EIGHTFOLD PATH CAN HELP US GET THERE

Eightfold, to us, is more than just a name. It's a philosophy. The Eightfold Path is a Buddhist teaching that maps the journey to nirvana, or enlightenment. It consists of eight areas that, if followed, will lead to awakening: right view, right resolve, right speech, right action, right livelihood, right effort, right mindfulness, and right concentration.

We believe the Eightfold Path can and should be applied to our careers, transforming them into something that nourishes our lives, rather than act as just a way to make ends meet.

We see our work as fundamental to creating positive change in people's lives. We thrive on people finding fulfilling work they genuinely enjoy. But it's not just about finding them the right role. We believe there is an even greater purpose for our work.

It's no coincidence that the United States has a bad reputation for having little or no work-life balance. In 2015, Americans didn't use 658 million vacation days, according to Project Time Off.[36] People regularly eat lunch at their desks, or stay late to get even more work done. Frequent travel, which is expected in many roles, has proven to result in behavioral and mental health concerns, according to a study published in the Journal of Occupational and Environmental Medicine. Our current system has turned into something that pushes workers to their limits, draining their energy — and their spirits.

Something has to change.

It's no coincidence that the United States has a bad reputation for having little or no work-life balance. In 2015, Americans didn't use 658 million vacation days, according to Project Time Off.

---

[36] https://projecttimeoff.com/press-releases/americans-waste-record-setting-658-million-vacation-days/

We envision a future of work more like the Eightfold Path: a culture that is balanced in positive interactions and experiences — creating a career that leads to personal fulfillment, not just a paycheck.

One way to create more meaning at work is through mentorship. It enhances job satisfaction while being philanthropic, helping both the mentor and the mentee. At Eightfold, we introduced Cultivate, a program that aims to give back through mentorship.

Since we are in the business of matching people to meaningful career paths, we want our employees to extend their experience to others. This includes helping college students with their resumes, making introductions in our network to help people land the jobs they are pursuing, and career counseling.

We encourage employees to invest their time, offer our office space, and reimburse them for reasonable expenses that help others. If everyone helped eight people (our magic number), we think we'd all be on the path towards a more enlightened workforce and ultimately, a better society at large.

Free lunches, naps pods, and pool tables are nice to have, but there's a deeper cultural problem in American workplaces. Company culture is more than just gimmicks that get people in the door. If you don't truly value your talent, they will leave.

In fact, employee turnover is the highest it's been in a decade[37].

That's because there needs to be a shift not only in the definition of talent management, but in the definition of 'talent' itself. Talent is exactly that — highly-trained, accomplished individuals. It's not people who work for a living, but skilled assets to your business. If people are not recognized appropriately, they will leave, or never come work for you in the first place.

Valuing your talent is about more than just creating engaging programs to foster professional and personal goals, although that is a step in the right direction. It's about respecting their opinions and recommendations, listening to their input, and ensuring their hard work does not go unnoticed.

In today's tight labor market it's not just recommended, it's imperative to remember: Your employees are your biggest assets.

AI AS A PLATFORM FOR CAREER GUIDANCE

AI doesn't just stop at helping you hire, it will also act as a tool for career guidance, adding further value for you and your top talent. As we've discussed before, resumes are inadequate at this stage of fast-paced change, and job descriptions are often even worse.

---

[37] https://www.forbes.com/sites/jeffboss/2018/02/26/employee-turnover-is-the-highest-its-been-in-10-years-heres-what-to-do-about-it/

We also discussed at length in our skills chapter (see **Chapter 4: The Half-Life of Skills is Shrinking Fast** for more) that as technology progresses rapidly, skill sets can become obsolete within a few years or less. Even if you stay in the same profession or industry, the nature of your role is changing rapidly. That makes staying relevant professionally difficult and can make your future path feel uncertain.

AI can help. This highly precise technology can help people visualize their career paths by identifying their strengths and applying those to other roles, mapping out a road for the future based on your transferable skills, not on specific learned methods. Things are changing too fast for us to keep up, so we must learn what our strengths are and where else they can be applied.

"When I graduated from college, programming was Pascal and Cobol. If you are graduating college today, you probably have not even heard of those languages," said Ashu Garg, a General Partner at Foundation Capital and board member at Eightfold. "We've got to help people visualize career paths. Then you've got to help people understand what the set of skills are they have to acquire. Those skills will no longer be acquired just by going to college for degrees, because the pace of change is so rapid, that whatever you've learned five or ten years ago is irrelevant."

It's up to you as an individual to learn new things and stay relevant, and we encourage business leaders to make ongoing professional education opportunities a priority. But AI can assist you here as well in identifying where your skills gaps are and analyzing how your accomplishments will help you in the future — often in new and unexpected ways. Once you've determined the skills you need, AI can help identify the steps you should take to reach your goal, or can give you a new objective by showing you where your skills apply in different fields.

Identifying adjacent experiences mean that your professional options open up, which is critical for companies that want to retain top talent as they move up, around, and over.

"This may be an engineer who has a certain skill set, but that actually translates really well to something that is something that is quite similar," said Mike Podobnik, Vice President, Global Talent & Employee Experience at Medallia, a software-as-a-service Customer Experience Management company based in San Mateo, California.

"If you are open to someone learning, you can actually go faster, you can broaden your talent pool, and you can find success where you might not otherwise. So in the scenario where the talent market it getting tighter and tighter, where there are more open jobs than there are qualified individuals, the idea of Eightfold being able to open that talent pool and shorten the length of a search, the implications of that for a company, for a team, for an individual, are really significant."

THE CHANGING ROLE OF THE HR MANAGER

As the nature of hiring changes, so too does the function of a talent manager. Because of the sheer quantity of applicants applying for coveted positions today at top companies, a huge part of today's talent management role has to be essentially 'busy work.' As Garg of Foundation Capital puts it: "The vast majority of people in HR today are just moving the process along."

"Recruiters spend hours a day just managing scheduling, collecting feedback, moving the process along," Garg added. "That work has to be automated so they can spend their time being talent managers."

With Eightfold, that work *is* automated. But rather than putting recruiters out of a job, it just means the role is evolving. The hours spent on so-called busywork can be used more effectively. This is an opportunity to think creatively and establish systems to ensure employees are having the best experience possible.

Monika Fahlbusch, an experienced HR executive, is the former Chief Employee Officer at BMC software, where she was responsible for all the back-office experiences of being an employee of BMC.

"I believe the way we work inside our companies is in need of disruption, particularly digital disruption," she said. "Most companies are facing challenges of either growing at scale, managing digital services, trying to get employees productive faster and differentiating themselves in the talent marketplace by integrating all these teams together so that the employee has one coordinated digital experience."

That digital transformation is a sign of what's to come in the future, she said. But her role was about much more than just filling seats faster. She believes great talent management takes imagination.

"You have to be technically curious. You have to have a disruptive mindset and you have to really think creatively about what is changing: what do we need to be doing differently?" Fahlbusch said. "So much of HR is process and policy and that can just be incredibly time consuming. You're never done, but I think really good chief people officers and CHROs need to spend as much time thinking creatively and innovatively and disrupting those, or they're going to lose."

Eightfold gives you that time. We want you to win. In fact, we want every at-bat to count.

Technology is increasing at such a rate that we, as humans, can hardly keep up. Some people may fear that by introducing artificial intelligence to an industry that has such a human touch we are rendering human resource managers useless. They're wrong. AI automates the dreary work of HR leaving more time for hiring managers to be human. It increases exposure to the parts of the job that get people excited in the first place; the human interaction, creating organizational systems and finding the perfect candidate for the right role.

Joel Torres is the Lead Talent Sourcer for the Diversity & Pipelines division at Twilio in Austin, Texas, and understands how this might be a frightening concept to some in his field.

"I think generally the industry is afraid of things like AI because they think it's going to do away with their job in the future," he said. "In the end I think it's only going to help. The person who can use all these different tools, use all these different programs to make hires, is going to be incredibly valuable in the future. And I think it's going to be the way to recruit in the future because it's going to take me from making five hires a month to 15."

Plus, we're only just beginning. The capabilities of AI in improving talent acquisition and management processes are only just being discovered, tested, expanded, and improved.

"I think that people who might be afraid of that and kind of shy away from AI in our industry are really going to be the ones who fall behind," Torres added.

THRIVING WITH GEN Z

As of 2017, millennials are the largest generation in the workforce. It seems the days of boomers' professional domination is over. But as millennials rise to positions of power in business, there is an even newer generation emerging. Although it has yet to be officially named, the group born after 1996 is often known as Gen-Z, iGen, or even post-millennials.

Millennials grew up in the internet explosion, a fact that has shaped their consumption of information and changed the way work is performed.

But even compared to the millennials who came before them, Gen-Z is the most diverse generation to date[38], according to Nielsen, and are coming of age without many of the events that defined the previous generation. They are growing up in an entirely different world from their predecessors. Even the youngest millennials remember a time of dial-up internet, Blockbuster as a cultural institution, and no smartphones.

To put it in perspective, the oldest post-millennial was 10 or 11 years old when the first iPhone was released. To them, "Angry Birds" is a way of life.

Michael Dimock, an analyst for the Pew Research Center, explains that technology is a given for post-millennials.[39]

---

[38] https://www.nielsen.com/us/en/insights/news/2017/youth-movement-gen-z-boasts-the-largest-most-diverse-media-users-yet.html
[39] *Defining generations: Where Millennials end and post-Millennials begin.* Retrieved from: http://www.pewresearch.org

For Gen Z, constant connectivity is a way of life

"By the time they were in their teens, the primary means by which young Americans connected with the web was through mobile devices, WiFi and high-bandwidth cellular service," he writes in a March 2018 report. "Social media, constant connectivity and on-demand entertainment and communication are innovations millennials adapted to as they came of age. For those born after 1996, these are largely assumed."

Maturing under today's circumstances means a whole new workforce we have to adapt to, and already companies are starting to notice. The oldest Gen-Zs have already graduated from college and are actively entering the professional world.

Kevin Dooney, senior director of the global digital workplace at BMC Software, has already seen the next generation's effect on some corporations. "I was at a conference with the folks at Microsoft and they're seeing younger people are no longer really getting their driver's licenses," he said. "So Microsoft in Canada is moving their headquarters out of the suburbs and into the city center of Toronto so they can tap into that talent. It's an interesting concept that the behaviors of an entire generation are shifting like that."

How will post-millennials shake things up further as they enter the workforce in masses? We can't wait to find out and be there to support you — and them — along the way.

THE FUTURE IS NOW

One by one, technology has revolutionized every industry. It started with transport during the industrial revolution, right to e-commerce with the rise of the internet. Up until now, hiring has remained largely untouched. Yes, computers and access to the internet have helped to simplify the application process for some, but the way we hire has remained stagnant for decades.

What we've discovered by creating Eightfold changes everything.

Will you join us and be a part of that change?

TOP TALENT TIPS

1. Implement a "Cultivate" program in your organization. At Eightfold, we encourage employees to invest their time, offer our office space and reimburse them for reasonable expenses that help others. If every one of your employees helped eight people (our magic number), think of how substantial the impact could be in expanding your company's mission and values.

2. Switch from an employer-centric to an employee-centric mindset.

3. Walk the talk. Try a different role yourself in your organization for a week or two. Take a task that you have to complete and see what one of your employees will need to go through to feel good about their contributions every day.

Acknowledgments

ACKNOWLEDGMENTS

This book would not have been possible without the generous help of our many talented colleagues, customers, employees, and board members. We'd like to thank all of you for your endless insights, well of knowledge, and continued support.

Thank you to all of those who shared their wisdom with us in interviews and during our panel talks and events. Not only was your expertise invaluable, but your passion and ideas continue to inspire us (who knows if this will lead to another book in the near future!). A special thank you to Aubrey Blanche, Nisha Biswal, Rajeev Butani, Glen Cathey, Daniel Doody, Ciara Ennis, Monika Fahlbusch, Ashu Garg, Kelly O. Kay, James Kinney, Jared Lucas, Cherrie McKinnon, Ashish Mediratta, Peter Nieh, Elle Odysseos, Mike Podobnik, Don Robertson, Michael Ross, Joel Torres, Sona Venkat, and Russell Williams.

To our co-founder Varun Kacholia, we are grateful everyday for your hard work, dedication, and leadership.

We are also indebted to our Eightfold.ai advisory board, individuals who constantly support and motivate us, and without whom there would be no Eightfold.

This book is the product of many months of hard work, but the creation of Eightfold itself is the result of years of research and dedication. We must credit our employees and customers for our success; thank you for all you have done to support us and all you continue to do. Our dream of revolutionizing talent management is impossible without you.

To everyone who has helped us on this journey, we are grateful. This book means so much to us; not only does it represent the thoughts and knowledge of so many talent management and AI experts, but we wholeheartedly believe in its message. We think meaningful employment is the backbone of our society. Everyone deserves the right career and can find it with the Eightfold path. Eightfold.ai was created to find the right person for the right role at the right time by working towards eliminating human bias and creating more intelligent, automated matchmaking throughout the talent journey from candidate to alumna. This is our mission. This gets us going every morning. Join us. Let's make the change we wish to see happen.

CPSIA information can be obtained
at www.ICGtesting.com
Printed in the USA
LVHW032353060320
649292LV00004B/168